JOHN CHIDLEY

Discovering
Book Collecting

Second, enlarged edition

SHIRE PUBLICATIONS

British Library Cataloguing in Publication Data: Chidley, John Discovering book collecting. – 2nd enlarged ed. – (Discovering; 267) 1. Book collecting I. Title II. Book collecting 002'.075 ISBN 0 7478 0387 0

To DJC
'...the fate of all books depends upon your capacities and not of your heads alone, but of your purses...' (from the Shakespeare First Folio of 1623).

ACKNOWLEDGEMENTS
I am indebted to John Slaughter for his expert and painstaking photography, and to Clive and Wendy Roberts for the very real help and encouragement they have given me. I wish also to thank two particular ex-colleagues at Henry Sotheran Ltd: Robert Kirkman, for his many kindnesses and unfailing good humour; and Graham Nowland, who originally told me to write this book.

Published in 1998 by Shire Publications Ltd, Cromwell House, Church Street, Princes Risborough, Buckinghamshire HP27 9AA, UK.
Copyright © 1982 and 1998 by John Chidley. First edition 1982; reprinted 1983, 1986, 1989 and 1993; second edition 1998. Number 267 in the Discovering series. ISBN 0 7478 0387 0.
John Chidley is hereby identified as the author of this work in accordance with section 77 of the Copyright, Designs and Patents Act, 1988.

Printed in Great Britain by CIT Printing Services Ltd, Press Buildings, Merlins Bridge, Haverfordwest, Pembrokeshire SA61 1XF.

Contents

William Caxton's device incorporating the letters W and C and symbols for 74, the year (1474) in which he printed his first book, according to Flanders dating.

Preface

No civilised home can be without books. But many people who do accumulate a large collection still remain fearful of the early printed book or the first edition of their favourite author; they are untouched by the quaintness of antique typography, the luxury of a choice old leather binding or the beauty of an illustrated volume and instead spend their money on acquiring masses of the cheapest available reprints.

This book sets out to show that although original is usually best it is not always most expensive. I hope to persuade the beginner that he can possess a chosen book in the format in which it first appeared to the world and as its author must have handled it, that attractive bindings exist on old books for boys as well as on rare incunabula, and that finely illustrated books can be purchased by the collector of more modest means than the millionaires who accumulate medieval manuscripts.

However, I make no apology for noticing some very expensive books. It is surely part of the collector's education to study, understand and appreciate the influences which have directed authors, printers, artists and publishers of the past. So while he may not yet be able to afford a Kelmscott Chaucer, he will at least admire it, realise its importance and perhaps make an effort to secure a good facsimile.

These are guidelines only, and further study is of course a prerequisite for the knowledgeable collector – but the real business of book collecting is collecting and I recommend browsing in your nearest second-hand bookshop at the earliest opportunity.

1. Introduction to printing and terminology

This chapter explains briefly how a book is made, describing the printing of the sheets and how these are gathered and sewn up to form a complete volume. The names of book sizes are explained and also the formulae used in the bibliographies which every collector has to consult at some stage. Although books are now printed very differently from those in early times (and have been since the early years of the nineteenth century), most of the terminology used by book collectors derives from the hand-printing era and some understanding of it is essential.

The printing press

The printing press is an adaptation of the common household

A printer's workshop, from 'A Book of Trades' (1568). One pressman inks the type while the other lifts the newly printed sheet to place on the left-hand pile in front. In the background, the compositors are arranging the type. The lever for the platen can be seen centre right.

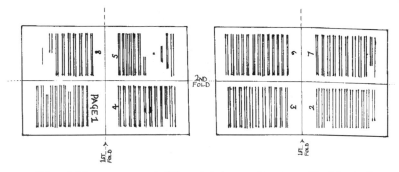

(Above) *The arrangement of the printed pages (i.e. imposition) for both sides of a single sheet. In this example there are eight printed pages. When the sheet is folded as shown, these pages will follow consecutively on four leaves – this is thus 'quarto format'.*

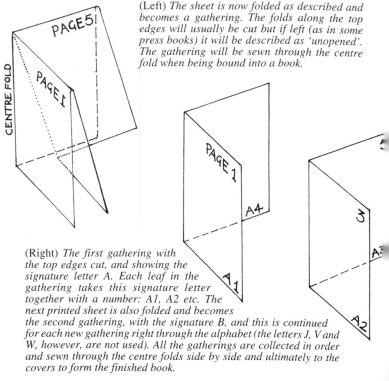

(Left) *The sheet is now folded as described and becomes a gathering. The folds along the top edges will usually be cut but if left (as in some press books) it will be described as 'unopened'. The gathering will be sewn through the centre fold when being bound into a book.*

(Right) *The first gathering with the top edges cut, and showing the signature letter A. Each leaf in the gathering takes this signature letter together with a number: A1, A2 etc. The next printed sheet is also folded and becomes the second gathering, with the signature B, and this is continued for each new gathering right through the alphabet (the letters J, V and W, however, are not used). All the gatherings are collected in order and sewn through the centre folds side by side and ultimately to the covers to form the finished book.*

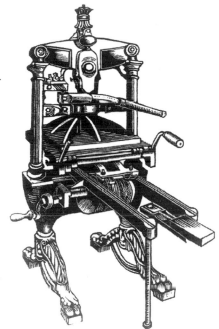

The Albion press, invented in 1822 by R. W. Cope, became immediately and lastingly popular owing to its simplicity and remains the preferred press of amateur printers. This wood engraving by Rosalind Bliss shows a press that was used at William Morris's Kelmscott Press.

press with two large pillars supporting a horizontal table or bed between them, on which the upright type is laid. Over this bed is a crossweight or *platen* which can be raised or lowered on to the type by means of a lever.

When any book is to be printed by hand the pages of the text have first to be made up and placed on the bed of the press. (Pages should not be confused with leaves; a page is one printed side of a leaf.) The separate letters or type are stored in order in a compartmented tray from which the *compositor* takes each letter as needed to build a word, and then a sentence, setting the type upside down and back to front in his composing stick. When the stick is full he transfers the type to a tray or *galley* and continues until he has completed a page. When four pages of text are completed they are arranged in the galley, secured with wedges and transferred to the bed of the printing press (face upwards) and inked by the pressman.

A sheet of paper is placed over the inked type and, by the pulling of a lever, the platen is lowered under pressure and squeezes the paper against the inked type to give an impression. The sheet of paper, now printed on one side, is left to dry, while the pressman continues to print off as many sheets of the same text as are required for the edition. He then receives a new set of four pages of text from the compositor and proceeds to print this new text on the blank sides of the sheets previously printed.

Format

All of these eight pages of text now spread over two sides of one sheet of paper and have been printed in what would appear to be random order, but when the sheet is folded into a *gathering* the pages follow consecutively. The *format* of the gathering illustrated, folded in half twice, with eight pages of print on four leaves, is *quarto*, and no matter how many of these gatherings are collected for the bound volume the format remains the same. A *folio* volume has gatherings of whole sheets folded in half once only with four pages of text on two leaves; and an *octavo* volume has gatherings of sheets folded in half three times to give sixteen pages of text on eight leaves.

Because sheets available to the printer from the paper mills used to be of standard sizes, the terms folio, quarto and octavo are often loosely used to denote the overall size of the finished volume, as well as its format. So a sheet size of $22\frac{1}{2}$ inches by

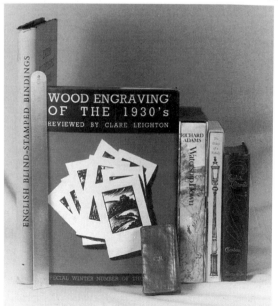

Nowadays it is more the shape and look of a book rather than its format or a strict adherence to inches that determine the size-name given. Left to right: folio, quarto, royal octavo, demy octavo, crown octavo, and in front a duodecimo, which at 4 inches tall almost qualifies as a miniature.

$17^{1}/_{2}$ inches folded in half once will give a folio of $17^{1}/_{2}$ inches by $11^{1}/_{4}$ inches, and folded in half once again will give a quarto of $11^{1}/_{4}$ inches by $8^{1}/_{4}$ inches, and all folios and quartos folded from this sheet size will have the same dimensions.

Table of book sizes

As explained above, nowadays these names are very often used solely for convenience, that is to say that the *size* of a modern novel may approximate to crown octavo even if its *format* is not.

Folio or 2º. Large, upright volumes, commonly the size used for atlases.

Crown folio	15 x 10 inches
Demy folio	$17^{1}/_{2}$ x $11^{1}/_{4}$ inches

Quarto or 4to. Large but square volumes, the typical 'coffee-table' art book.

Crown 4to	10 x $7^{1}/_{2}$ inches
Demy 4to	$11^{1}/_{4}$ x $8^{3}/_{4}$ inches
Royal 4to	$12^{1}/_{2}$ x 10 inches

Octavo or 8vo. The commonest size: *crown 8vo* for novels and *demy 8vo* for biographies.

Crown 8vo	$7^{1}/_{2}$ x 5 inches
Demy 8vo	$8^{3}/_{4}$ x 5 inches
Royal 8vo	10 x $6^{1}/_{4}$ inches

Smaller books with more complicated foldings may be 12mo or duodecimo, with twelve leaves in a gathering; 16mo or sextodecimo, with sixteen leaves; or even 32mo or trigesimosecundo, with thirty-two (pronounced respectively 'twelve-mow', 'sixteen-mow' and 'thirty-two-mow').

Collation in bibliographies

Each gathering in a book is given a *signature* letter A-Z and each leaf in the gathering is also numbered. This means that any one particular leaf can immediately be described by bibliographers. Instead of saying 'the leaf on which unnumbered pages 3 and 4 are printed is torn, page 3 stained', he can

115. Hunting of the Snark (1876) [89

THE HUNTING | OF THE SNARK | an 𝔄gonꭒ, | in 𝔈ight 𝔉its. ||
BY | LEWIS CARROLL | AUTHOR OF "ALICE'S ADVENTURES IN
WONDERLAND," AND "THROUGH THE | LOOKING-GLASS," || *WITH
NINE ILLUSTRATIONS* | BY | HENRY HOLIDAY ||

London: Macmillan and Co.: 1876: (fours) 8°: size 7$^1/_8$ × 4$^{13}/_{16}$ in.: pp.
[xiv] + 84 + [2], signn, [*a*], *b*, B–L⁴, [M]². CONTENTS: p. i, half-title | The
Hunting of the Snark | : iv, frontispiece: v, title, as above and at foot: [*The
Right of Translation and Reproduction is Reserved*.]: vi, imprint in the centre,
London: R. Clay, Sons and Taylor, Printers, Bread Street Hill. | vii, three
lines of dedication 'to a dear Child' over four four-line stanzas, see below:
ix–xi, preface: [xiii] list of contents, in Eight Fits or Chapters: each Fit or
Chapter has a half-title and a following blank page: 1–83, the poem: [84]
imprint, exactly as on p. vi, above: [1] blank except for | [Turn over. | at the
bottom right-hand corner: [2] Macmillan's advertisements of Lewis Carroll's works, with press opinions.

Generally issued in buff-coloured cloth, dark-grey end-papers. Black
lettering along the back, | The. Hunting. of. the. Snark | The front cover has
six black lines around the border, broken by ten circles at equal intervals,
the space within these lines is devoted entirely to a picture of the Bellman
on the yard-arm of a ship, a large sail on the mast bears the words | The |
Hunting | of the | Snark | all printed in black. The back cover has the same
border, but the picture in the centre is that of a bell buoy in a rough sea
bearing the words | It | Was | a | Boojum |. All edges gilt.

*A very thorough bibliographical description of an older book from 'The
Lewis Carroll Handbook' (revised edition D. Crutch, Dawson, 1979). The
transcription of the titlepage is quasi-facsimile to give an idea of what it
looks like and the double or triple bar || is used to show that there is more
space than usual between the lines. There follows the publisher, date (with
further information as to the day and month in the succeeding notes),
format ('in fours' means that the folded sheet of 8 leaves has been split into
two gatherings of 4 for binding), then cover measurements, numeration of
pages (and note from the square brackets that the first 14 and the last 2 are
not numbered), signatures, contents and binding, after which (not shown)
is a detailed account of the circumstances surrounding publication.*

say 'A2 torn, recto stained'. (*Recto* is the top or front of the leaf
and *verso* the back – thus in any open book the page on the left
will be a verso and that on the right a recto.)

This formula also means that the bibliographer can quickly
note down the collation of any volume for reference. For
example, the make-up of Thomas Hardy's volume of poems
called *Winter Words* may be described by listing the pages: pp
[I]-[XII] 1-202 [203-04]; but more compactly as [A]⁶ B-N⁸ O⁶.

This means that gathering A has six leaves and each of the twelve gatherings B to N has eight leaves (the signature letters J, V and W are always omitted by convention) and the final gathering O has six leaves. The square brackets in the formula are used to denote that the number or letter within is not actually printed on the leaf for some reason, but it may be assumed.

Signatures were introduced to let the binder see at a glance if he had arranged the gatherings in the correct order, but modern binding machines do not require them, and where they are absent the bibliographer must use pagination for his collation.

In bibliographies the titlepage of the book described is always given in full so that careful comparison may be made and it is a convention that an oblique dash or vertical bar marks the end of a line. The titlepage of the Hardy volume described

A bibliographical description of a modern book from Fifoot's 'Soho Bibliography of the Sitwells', 1971. There are a couple of things to note: firstly, in keeping with modern practice for modern books, neither the format nor the signatures (if there are any) are given, just the cover size and pagination. Note also from the transcription that the titlepage itself is not dated and that, in spite of the fact that the publisher has printed 'First Published in 1945' on the verso, Mr Fifoot knows from other sources that it was actually published in 1946 and so puts the date within square brackets in the main entry.

---

oA37   THE TRUE STORY OF   [1946]
DICK WHITTINGTON

First edition

THE TRUE STORY OF | DICK WHITTINGTON | A CHRIST-
MAS STORY FOR CAT-LOVERS | BY | OSBERT SITWELL |
LONDON | HOME & VAN THAL LTD. | 3 CLIFFORD
STREET. W.1

182 × 119 mm.

48 pp.: [1] half-title; [2] blank; [3] title; [4] "First Published 1945. . . . Printed by The Chaseton Press of H. Williams & Son Ltd., 222 Grays Inn Road, London, W.C.1"; [5] 6–48 text.

Terra-cotta cloth boards. Trimmed edges. Lettered in black on upper cover.

Published in February 1946 at 5s.

11

above would be transcribed WINTER WORDS/IN VARIOUS MOODS AND METRES/BY/THOMAS HARDY/ MACMILLAN AND CO, LIMITED/ST MARTIN'S STREET, LONDON/1928, from which it will be seen that there are seven lines. Most bibliographies will go on to note binding and other relevant physical attributes.

When the gatherings are sewn together the volume is either casebound in cloth or boards, as are most modern books, or bound by craftsmen in the traditional way, sewn on cords with covers of leather. In the binding the *forwarder* does the collating, sewing and covering and the *finisher* stamps the lettering on the spine and adds any decorations on the covers of the book in real gold leaf. Paperbacks are usually not sewn (although this volume is) but the inside edges are trimmed square and a pliable gum solution (*gutta-percha* or *caoutchouc*) is applied, on to which the spine and covers can be stuck.

(Left) *The badge of the oldest of the booksellers' associations and* (right) *the logo, designed by Edward Bawden, of a newer one, founded in 1974, the Provincial Booksellers Fairs Association.*

2. Practical experience

The trite saying that experience is the best teacher applies as truly to book collecting as to anything, but the beginner can take certain precautions to ensure that the mistakes he will assuredly make will not be disastrous, and the most obvious precaution is to know and be known by the booksellers in his area. Not only will they be more eager to report wanted books to the regular collector, but they will be more ready to advise about the peculiarities, scarcity and desirability of books which the collector may be about to purchase.

Most booksellers after the minimum of three years in business apply to join the Antiquarian Booksellers' Association, which sets the standards for fair and honest trading as well as organising the Antiquarian Book Fair every summer in London; its members will display the ABA badge in their shops and usually in their catalogues. Other more frequent book fairs throughout Britain are organised by the Provincial Booksellers Fairs Association; these are advertised in the press and should not be missed.

Buying from a bookseller's catalogue is obviously less satisfactory than buying from the shelf, but for most working people the former course is inevitable, and in any case many booksellers

A section from a bookseller's catalogue.

---

394 WAUGH (Evelyn). The Ordeal of Gilbert Pinfold, First Edition, *post 8vo.* original blue cloth, £12. 1957
    Near fine in dust-jacket.

395 WELLS (H. G.). The Time Machine, an invention, First Edition, *post 8vo.* original cream cloth, uncut, £68. 1895
    With a 32-page catalogue of publisher's advertisements.
    Wells's fourth published work, but his first science fiction novel.
    From the library of C. H. C. 'Harry' Pirie-Gordon, scholar, author and friend of Frederick Rolfe 'baron Corvo', with his bookplate.
    Covers dust marked otherwise a very good copy.

396 WELLS (H. G.). Meanwhile, The Picture of a Lady, First Edition, *post 8vo.* original brown cloth, in dust-jacket, £8.50. 1927

397 WHISTLER (Lawrence). The Emperor Heart, First Edition, with decorations by Rex Whistler, *8vo.* original purple cloth, £18. 1936

---

will keep their choicest plums for first display in a prestigious list. Some care is needed, however, and all descriptions should be fully and carefully read before an order is placed. Familiarity with the cataloguer's usage and with the reputation of his firm will be a decided advantage, and remember that there is room for considerable difference of opinion over such apparently categorical terms as 'near-fine', 'very good copy' and 'fresh and sound'.

Original state

It is nowadays usually considered that whenever possible books should be purchased in original state, that is retaining the physical form in which they appeared on publication day. For modern first editions in original cloth this is not difficult, but the keen collector will also expect his copies to have dustjackets.

With older books the situation is less clear-cut. A Jacobean Bible in contemporary panelled calf is not uncommon, but a Shakespeare folio would be (they are usually choicely bound in Victorian full morocco). Sir Walter Scott's novels were published in grey boards but will now probably be in Regency half calf or even Edwardian morocco, and Dickens's works were published in monthly parts, which are expensive, because they are difficult to find complete, and are awkward to store; in this case the collector will probably find a contemporary publisher's half morocco or calf a perfectly acceptable alternative.

Condition

A book's condition is a factor often not sufficiently considered by the novice, but he should early in his career decide to abide by the cardinal rule never to make do with a poor or incomplete volume except where a better copy is not to be procured. A first edition of *Nicholas Nickleby* lacking the engraved portrait frontispiece of Dickens, with the plates badly foxed and the joints on the cover broken, would hardly be a bargain at any price.

Generally the older a book is and the more popular it has been, the less fastidious the collector can afford to be about condition. Any volume printed by Caxton, even if hopelessly incomplete, is valuable and any seventeenth-century edition of Bunyan's *Pilgrim's Progress* (1678) will be hotly competed for, be it thumbed, browned, dog-eared or even damp-stained, all very likely with such a popular work.

Particular faults are to be expected in certain types of book or even in individual titles; thus the fine steel-engraved views in Bartlett's *American Scenery* (1832) will almost certainly be a little foxed in the margins (and there will probably be some offsetting on to the text) and the fragile lettering used on the spine of H. G. Wells's *History of Mr Polly* (1910) will usually be chipped. Most collectors will accept these defects, knowing that any remarkable copies which have survived without them will command a considerably higher price.

The gradations in describing condition usually follow this pattern:

Mint or *immaculate*: as new, in dustjacket if called for.
Fine or *very fine*: just off new condition, little sign of use.
Nice or *good*: a bright, clean and sound second-hand copy.
Poor or *used*: may be thumbed, stained or marked but this will be stated; usually qualified 'used but sound'.
Working copy: lowest in the pecking order, it may just be acceptable for a much wanted reference book.

Apart from the self explanatory *pristine*, the condition of a binding is often mentioned only when there are defects, e.g. 'rubbed, leather peeling, joints tender or cracked but sound, covers detached' (this would need rebacking), and so on.

Book care

Unlike some collectable objects, most books are not fragile and are meant to be handled, admired and read; but they cannot take careless treatment for long without damage. A book should be taken from the shelf by its sides, not winkled out by the top of the spine with a finger; it should be held in the palm of the hand with both covers supported since nothing cracks joints more quickly than letting one cover drop. Books should be shelved so that they fit snugly but not tightly, and away from direct sunlight, which will fade and possibly rot the spine (the bindings in the great library at Blenheim Palace were found to be badly perished when that collection was sold in 1881), and, ideally, protected from the sulphur-filled pollution of the city.

Dr Johnson is supposed to have dusted his books by banging them together, but a soft rag is to be preferred, and regular handling will prevent damp taking hold. If dampness is detected, usually in the form of small pink mould growths accompanied by a musty smell, the books affected should be left standing in warm circulating air, after which the mould can be wiped away with a clean cloth. Any more drastic treatment should be left to experts, who can also best deal with the all but extinct bookworm.

It is a good idea occasionally to treat leather-bound books with a lubricant. The special dressing formulated by the British Library Laboratories is still available but should be used sparingly since it contains hexane, which in very large doses may be harmful to leather. An alternative is the traditional forty per cent neatsfoot oil and sixty per cent anhydrous lanolin, sparsely applied (soak a piece of cotton wool, then wring almost dry), giving particular attention to the joints. After this the book should be left to dry, then carefully rubbed to polish off the remaining oil.

Dirty leather or vellum bindings may be carefully washed, using a damp (not wet) sponge with a little soap and gently rubbing over the whole area, taking care that the surface of the skin and the dye are not disturbed. A soft rag should be used to remove all soap before drying, after which the lubricant may be applied as described above.

Repairs

Some simple repair jobs can be done at home; for example, odd loose leaves or plates can be tipped back into place using a water-based paste (not whole sections, which must be sewn back in). But when substantial repair seems necessary it is essential to seek advice from a well established binder or bookshop. Usually the binder will require specific instructions for each job and here the collector's own good taste and judgement must come into play. The original binding should be preserved where possible, so that if a volume needs rebacking the binder may be able to incorporate the original spine on the new or at least mimic the original period tooling. An experienced binder will not need to be told to stain his new spine to the colour of the original; to supply old-style headbands and only if necessary new endpapers; to provide inside cloth joints for heftier books; and *at all costs* to avoid cropping the margins of the book.

Prices

Any word about prices will so quickly be outdated that it is perhaps a subject in which the collector is best left to educate himself by browsing in bookshops and booksellers' and auctioneers' catalogues. The published guides to prices rarely consider condition or notice special provenances, association or binding on the books they list, and they are therefore price indicators of the vaguest kind. For example, a copy of the first edition of the first James Bond book, *Casino Royale* (1954), might fetch a certain price, but a mint copy in the dustjacket, inscribed by the author, Ian Fleming, to Sir Maurice Oldfield (the supposed model for 'M') would be a prime association copy and might sell for twenty or thirty times more.

Fashion is an important factor to reckon with in book collecting and good authors or subjects which are out of fashion (Thackeray, Tennyson, theology, great histories, archaeology and so on) may be collected with advantage both with regard to prices and availability. It is an often heard complaint that 'I wish I had properly collected detective fiction, or G. A. Henty, when they were to be had for a song'. The true collector will find most satisfaction (it might almost be called a duty) in determining his own area of interests outside the mainstream of collecting and uncovering for himself and for future collectors and bibliographers the important and pioneering works, as well as the trifles, in his chosen field.

3. The history of early printing

Before the fifteenth century all books had to be laboriously handwritten and were consequently expensive and in short supply. Although there were scriptoria in which a large number of scribes might work all day long copying this or that text for orders received, it was a lengthy and tedious business and by the middle of the century was hardly adequate to cope with the demands of an increasingly literate public. So it was that a number of inventive people were endeavouring, at around the same time, to perfect the quicker and less costly method of producing books by mechanical means.

Johann Gutenberg

Johann Gutenberg (1400-68), a goldsmith of the city of Mainz on the Rhine, was the first to solve the problem satisfactorily, and he did it not only by mastering the art of printing, that is the operation of taking impressions on paper from inked type, which was already known in the ancient Far East, but by inventing the technology to cast his type in the first place. With this newly cast type (called *movable* since it can be dismantled and reused) and the adapted presses in his shop, Gutenberg printed his first book in 1455. It was a folio Latin Bible of over six hundred pages printed in double columns and, remarkably, this first printed book, the first edition of the Bible, is also amongst the most magnificent of all printed books.

In the physical job of printing the Bible Gutenberg had relied heavily on his foreman, Peter Schöffer, while the financial backing for the project had come from Johann Fust, but as the Bible came off the press these two turned against Gutenberg. Fust sued him for the return of the loan, and Gutenberg, unable to pay, was made to forfeit all of his printing equipment, including some new types, to Fust, who now took over the business with Schöffer as his partner. After this unsavoury incident Gutenberg quietly disappeared from the limelight, although he did receive a good pension from the church and may have been the printer of an immense dictionary, the *Catholicon* in 1460.

Other prototypographers

The first fruit of the collaboration between Fust and Schöffer is the Psalter of 1457, which, with its large gothic type and superb lombardic initials printed in red and blue, remains one

The device of Fust and Schöffer, 1462.

of the most beautiful of all books; it is also the first book to give both the names of the printers and the date of printing. This enterprising pair also produced the first book with a printer's mark, the Bible of 1462, the first printed classic, Seneca, in 1463, and the first titlepage proper, on a Papal Bull of the same year.

It was not to be expected that printing with movable type would long remain secret and the art spread rapidly from Mainz to other German cities and thence to other countries. The earliest printers, all German, seem to have been remarkably intelligent and innovative men and took considerable commercial risks in setting up their presses in new towns. Some famous names are: Johann Mentelin, who issued the first German Bible in 1466; Albrecht Pfister, who published *Der Edelstein* (Aesop's Fables), the first illustrated book, in Bamberg in 1461; Sweynheym and Pannartz, the first printers in Italy in 1465; and Erhard Ratdolt, who printed the first edition of Euclid's *Geometry* at Venice in 1482.

Gothic or black letter and roman type

The earliest printers had copied the manuscript writing of the professional German scribes when designing their types, and these were very angular and rather constricted, and they gave the page a very black appearance. But from the middle of the

pl⁹ irritat. furoꝛē dei puocat. irā dei indignāter pl⁹
fibi exagitat . q̇ ꝓo patiēter aduerfa tolerat deū fibi
citius placat.hec ille. Et ideo inimicū aut pfecutoꝛē

(Above) *Black letter.* (Below) *Roman type; notice how each of the angles on the letter forms have been rounded off in the roman type below.*

minas nō tm̄ doctis nota funt:fꝫ expmunt etiā
tant:ut fint oībus notiora?Poffunt ne int bꝫc
etiā fi natura fint boni:ab ipfis tn̄ dijs erudian

fifteenth century Italian scribes had developed a much rounder and more legible writing, the capitals of which were based on Roman epigraphy and the minuscules on the Carolingian script. This new style was copied by the early Italian printers and seemed particularly suitable for the many classical texts then being resurrected.

That roman was the more successful typeface, so that it is now used almost exclusively for all printed books, is due largely to its greater legibility and to its active promotion by two of the greatest printers ever.

Nicolaus Jensen

Nicolaus Jensen (1420-80) was a French diecutter who learned to print in Germany and arrived in Venice in 1468, when he may have cut types for the first Venetian printer, de Spira. In 1470 he printed his own first book, *De Evangelica*, and he had produced fifty-four other titles by his death in 1480. Jensen cut all his own type, designing roman faces which have been described in glowing terms by every typographer and bibliophile from Dibden and William Morris to Updike and Rogers. They have become a standard for true roman which all subsequent designers have tried to emulate. Jensen's most celebrated books are the Pliny *Naturalis Historia* and the Diogenes *Vitae*, both of 1475.

Aldus Manutius

Aldus Manutius (1450-1515) was the original scholar-printer and his press, with its anchor and dolphin device first used in an edition of Dante in 1502, is the most celebrated of all. His remarkable and unparalleled publishing career started in Venice in 1490 when he began preparations to issue scholarly texts of previously unpublished classical authors: Aristotle in 1495, Aristophanes in 1498, Herodotus and Sophocles in 1502, Plato and Pindar in 1513 and so on. His books became renowned throughout Europe for their quality, reliability and handsome printing.

Aldus was fortunate to attract a brilliant typographer, Francesco Griffo, to his business, and Griffo's greatest contribution to the Aldine press was the design of a small cursive type which would allow the great classics to be issued in pocket size and yet be readable and elegant. The first volume printed in the new type was a Virgil of 1501, but so great was its success that it was used over and over again and widely copied. In England it was called italic after its country of origin and it is still used by every printer, *as these last words show.*

Incunabula

All these books printed up to and including the somewhat arbitrary date of 1500 are called *incunables* or *incunabula* (a word derived from the Latin for 'from the cradle', since these are the 'cradle books' of printing).

Although it is estimated that some forty thousand different editions of books were issued up to 1500, interest in the productions of the early presses has always been keen and high prices prevail (a copy of William Caxton's *The Canterbury Tales,* 1478, was sold for £4,600,000 in 1998). Some knowledge of them, however, is useful and even the collector of modest means can still obtain at reasonable prices examples of odd leaves from the early presses.

4. From Caxton to Dickens

William Caxton

One of the most celebrated of all Englishmen, William Caxton (1422-91) was a prosperous and influential mercer who was head of the contingent of English merchants trading in the duchy of Burgundy. He was already an accomplished translator of French courtly tales when in 1471 he decided to learn about the new craft of printing and travelled to Cologne, probably to the shop of Johann Veldener, where he helped to print an edition of *De Proprietatibus Rerum.*

Having purchased some types from Veldener, Caxton returned to Bruges and set to printing on his own account, his first book being a tale of the Trojan wars in 1475. Two other publications followed when Caxton, perhaps feeling his apprenticeship was truly over, moved to England and set up as a printer at the heraldic sign of the red pale in the precincts of Westminster Abbey, close to the busy chapter house, where he would come into regular contact with the wealthiest and most influential people in the land.

Caxton's first book in England was the *Dicts or Sayings of the Philosophers*, finished in November 1477, and during the next fourteen years he printed almost one hundred separate pieces, including the first edition of Chaucer's *The Canterbury Tales* in 1478 (with an illustrated edition in 1483), an illustrated Aesop in 1484, Voragine's *The Golden Legend* in 1484 (a massive collection of saints' lives translated by Caxton himself) and, perhaps most importantly of all, since for a long time Caxton's was the only known text, Malory's *Le Morte d'Arthur* in 1485. Caxton was primarily concerned with making his business pay, but he disseminated the classics of English as never before and his service to English literature is incalculable. He died in 1491 and his assistant, Wynkyn de Worde, then took over the business.

The sixteenth and seventeenth centuries

Two indispensable reference works fully list all English books published from Caxton to the year 1700. These are known as 'STC' and 'Wing' (see Bibliography) and should be consulted for any information on authors, the works they published, the number of editions printed and sometimes for the number of copies of any particular work which survive.

William Shakespeare (1564-1616) was little concerned in the publication of his own books, although, newly arrived in London, he did arrange for his Stratford friend Richard Field to print his first two books, *Venus and Adonis* in 1593 and *Lucrece* in 1594. The first edition (1609) of his *Sonnets,* some of which had been circulated, as was the custom, in manuscript, may have been piratically published, and certainly the second edition, *Poems,* of 1640, was printed without family authority, a fate suffered by most of his plays. The first was *Romeo and Juliet* in 1597, followed among others by *Henry V* and *The Merchant of Venice* in 1600, *Hamlet* in 1603 and *Othello* in 1622. These separately printed plays are known as quartos after their format and are usually imperfect and rough texts hastily copied from a live performance and equally hurriedly printed.

After Shakespeare's death two of his friends, John Heminge and Henry Condell, collected printed and manuscript copies which they thought accurate and issued a collected one-volume edition of his plays, modelling the volume on Ben Jonson's *Workes* of 1616. How far these texts were authentic is still debated, but of the thirty-six plays which they printed in the *first folio* of 1623 no fewer than eighteen had never before been published (including *Macbeth* and *The Tempest*) and might otherwise have been lost. Other Shakespeare folios followed in 1632, 1664 and 1685 and the first octavo edition was published by Nicholas Rowe in six volumes in 1709.

The attention of the world's collectors has been turned to Shakespeare for a very long time and all of the early editions are very expensive, but extracted plays from the second to fourth folios still occur for sale at modest prices, and even single leaves from one of the folios are not to be despised. There have been various facsimiles of the first folio: that issued in 1902 by the Oxford University Press is one of the best.

Other editions of Shakespeare can be of interest and may not be expensive. The edition published by Charles Knight in three volumes in 1843 had delightful illustrations by Kenny Meadows, and the *Globe Shakespeare* published by Macmillan in 1864 was the first one-volume complete Shakespeare in pocket size but is usually modestly priced.

Bibles

Printed scripture in English begins with the New Testament of William Tyndale, published in 1525, and the first complete Bible of 1535 by Miles Coverdale. Both are of very great rarity,

THE HOLY
BIBLE
Containing the Old
TESTAMENT,
and the New.
Newly tranſlated out
of the Original Tongues
And with the former
Tranſlations diligently
Compared, and
reviſed

Cambridge
Printed by John Field
Printer to ÿ Univerſitie.
1661.

POCULA SACRA HINC LUCEM
ALMA MATER CANTA BRIGIA

Prov. 9.1.

A handsome engraved titlepage (called 'architectural' because of the entablature) by Vaughan on an octavo Restoration Bible. Only Oxford and Cambridge universities and the king's printer in London were allowed to print Bibles.

those copies which escaped confiscation by the antagonistic authorities being read by their owners until they fell to pieces.

In 1560 a group of Calvinist exiles in Geneva made a new translation of the Bible from the Hebrew and Greek and for the first time divided the chapters into verses for easy study. This *Geneva Version* (or Breeches Bible after the reading in Genesis chapter 3 verse 7: '. . and they made themselves breeches'), cheaply printed and in manageable quarto format, became the most popular Bible of the day and was the version used by Shakespeare.

The celebrated *Authorised Version* was James I's official alternative to the Geneva Version and was first published in folio format in 1611. It was not until this too was issued in quarto format (1612) that it began first to rival and eventually to supplant the Geneva Version in popular esteem. Very often these Tudor and Jacobean Bibles have bound in with them a *Book of Common Prayer*, a *Concordance* or *The Genealogy of Christ* (with a map of the Holy Land by John Speed). Copies should be carefully checked as they are very often defective, being notorious for the absence of the preliminaries, although even incomplete copies are of interest.

Later Bibles are usually only of commercial value if they are finely printed, like the *Vinegar Bible* in two folio volumes (1716) or the *Maclin* six-volume folio Bible of 1800; or if they are important new translations, like the *Revised Standard Version* of 1881-5 in five volumes; or if they are in a choice contemporary leather binding. Old Victorian Bibles will not usually fall into any of these categories and are probably of little interest except as period pieces.

The eighteenth century

The outstanding literary character of the eighteenth century was Samuel Johnson (1709-84), whose great work was the *Dictionary of the English Language* published in two massive volumes in 1755; the last edition of this work revised by Johnson himself was the fourth of 1773. Johnson was a prolific and truly professional author, who edited two magazines, *The Rambler* (1750-2) and *The Idler* (1761), wrote a play, *Irene* (1749), and an oriental novel, *Rasselas*, in two volumes (1759) some twenty-six years before Beckford's *Vathek* (1786), as well as such miscellaneous pieces as the unsigned Preface to Percy's *Reliques of Antient English Poetry* (three volumes, 1765), a pioneering collection of antique ballads. He is best known through the writings of James Boswell, whose celebrated *Life of Samuel Johnson* appeared in two volumes in 1791, in an edition of 1750 copies, each with an engraved portrait of Johnson by Reynolds.

The eighteenth was also the century when the novel was discovered, prime examples being Henry Fielding's *Tom Jones* (six volumes, 1749) and Laurence Sterne's eccentric *Tristram Shandy* (nine volumes, York and London, 1760–7).

There is a great gulf in commercial terms between the established classics of the eighteenth century and the literature which mirrored the interests and concerns of everyday life. Sermons and theological disputes of the age are still almost given away although they may be early examples of a provincial imprint (many small towns at this time had their own printers) or be by a character of some local consequence, and they may have stimulated enormous controversy at the time of publication. Cheap reprints of the popular poetry and novels of the day are worth collecting as period pieces of book production.

Robert and Andrew Foulis

The Foulis brothers were Scotland's finest printers. Starting in Glasgow in 1742 with type purchased from Alexander Wilson, they soon became known for the elegance of their typography and the reliability of their texts, which were largely new editions of classical authors. They were appointed university printers in the following year. Their most famous books are the Horace of 1744 and Homer of 1758. Robert died in 1776 and Andrew in 1775, having printed some six hundred editions, but Robert's son continued the business until 1795. It was he who issued in 1788 the fine edition of Allan Ramsay's *The Gentle Shepherd* which contains some of the earliest aquatint plates published in Britain.

John Baskerville

John Baskerville (1706-75) was one of the first printers to take a passionate interest in all aspects of his trade. As a wealthy man, Baskerville, who like Caxton turned to printing in later life, was able to have all his own type cut (it was based on

A Baskerville decorative border.

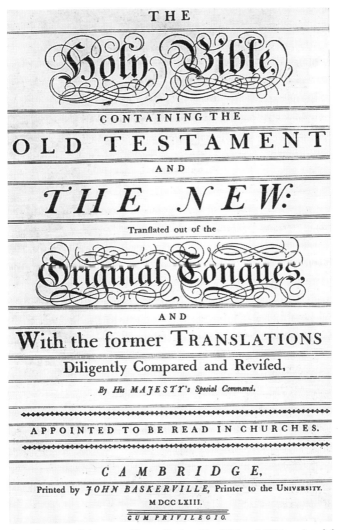

THE

Holy Bible

CONTAINING THE

OLD TESTAMENT

AND

THE NEW:

Tranſlated out of the

Original Tongues,

AND

With the former TRANSLATIONS

Diligently Compared and Reviſed,

By His MAJESTY's Special Command.

APPOINTED TO BE READ IN CHURCHES.

CAMBRIDGE,

Printed by JOHN BASKERVILLE, Printer to the UNIVERSITY.

M DCC LXIII.

CUM PRIVILEGIO.

The titlepage of the magnificent Baskerville Bible of 1763, printed for Cambridge University. The second and eighth lines are printed xylographically (from engraved wood blocks) and the straight rules between each line are added by hand in red ink, hence 'ruled in red'.

the Old Face design of the famous typefounder William Caslon (1692-1766) and also to experiment with new inks and special papers. His first book was an edition of Virgil published in 1757 and this was followed by various editions of Milton from 1758 (his new edition of *Paradise Regained*, 1759, is the first book printed on wove rather than laid paper), Addison's *Works* in four volumes (1761) and a series of beautifully printed *Books of Common Prayer* from 1760, some with a very elegant typographic border to each page (see page 26). His greatest work, however, is the handsome folio Bible printed at Cambridge for the University Press in 1763, although he issued another Bible in Birmingham in 1769. Baskerville is one of England's greatest printers but many of his books are still undervalued and may often be found in attractive contemporary bindings.

Stereotypes

An interesting innovation of the eighteenth century is the invention of stereotyping, firstly in Germany and Holland and later in Britain by William Ged (1690-1749), whose process involved taking plaster moulds of standing type and from that producing a metal plate. A publisher in those days had two options once his book had been printed: leave the type set up just as it was ('standing') in case a reprint was called for; or break up the type ('distribute'), and start on a new book with it, but this meant that any reprint would have to be re-composed from scratch. Neither option was entirely satisfactory, given the expense of type and labour, but now, with the whole book stored on metal plates, all he had to do was pull them out and reprint! But, as may be supposed, the printers were not enthusiastic about the invention and it was quietly ignored for over a hundred

Sallust's 'Histories' printed by William Ged in 1739: the first book printed from stereotype plates.

years, the only survivors being Ged's own *Sallust* of 1739 and the reprint of 1744.

Later, in Victorian times, the process was revived as being the quickest way to get the whole text of a newly published book by a bestselling author to a friendly New York publisher and thus beat the pirates, who would have to buy the book in London, cross the Atlantic, set it up and print; by which time the friendly publisher would have the book in the shops. Many first American editions of authors like Dickens, Thackeray and Hardy were printed in this way.

The nineteenth century

In literature the nineteenth is above all the century of the novel and the collector will be faced with acquiring them in three ways: as serials, in original parts or as three-deckers.

Three-deckers

The three-decker was the standard form in which most novels were published for almost the whole of the nineteenth century, that is in three separate volumes. Later on it was the great circulating libraries like Mudie's which kept the system alive because, published at a guinea or thirty shillings, the novels were usually too expensive for most people to buy and had to be borrowed. Consequently many three-deckers now surviving are former library copies, and therefore their condition is usually poor.

The three-decker owes its original success to Sir Walter Scott (1771-1832). His brain teeming with images from the border ballads which he so assiduously collected, Scott started the twenty-three historical tales which go under the general title of the Waverley Novels with *Waverley* itself in 1814. It was an immediate bestseller, with four reprints in the same year, and other titles followed in rapid succession: *Guy Mannering* (1815), *Rob Roy* (1818), *Ivanhoe* (1820) and *Kenilworth* (1821), all published anonymously in three volumes. Scott's books are still generally not hard to find, but it will be easier to collect them in contemporary half calf (probably without the half-titles) than in the fragile grey boards as originally issued.

Jane Austen (1775-1817), a contemporary of Scott, published the first of her six novels in 1811. This was *Sense and Sensibility*, which sold at fifteen shillings for the three volumes; probably only one thousand copies were printed. *Pride and Prejudice* followed in 1813, *Mansfield Park* in 1814, *Emma* in 1816 and *Northanger Abbey* and *Persuasion*, two novels in four volumes, were posthumously published in 1818.

So determined were the reading public and the libraries that the three-decker was the only appropriate format for a new novel that it is said that some authors had to pad out their story to fill the space: and when Emily Brontë found that *Wuthering Heights* would fill only two volumes, her sister Anne obliged with a separate short novel, *Agnes Grey*, to make up the third. They were published in 1847 as by 'Ellis' and 'Acton Bell'. Another sister, Charlotte, wrote *Jane Eyre* (1847), *Shirley* (1849) and *Villette* (1853), all pseudonymously, and *The Professor* in two volumes was posthumously published in 1857.

For the first time professional authors were making a lot of money from their books and one of the most successful was Anthony Trollope (1815-82). Of his huge output, the loosely knit Barsetshire novels are best known. These start with *The Warden* in one volume (1855) and proceed with *Barchester Towers* (1857), *Doctor Thorne* (1858), *Framley Parsonage* (1861), all in three volumes, and then *The Small House at Allington* (1864) and *The Last Chronicle of Barset* (1867), both in two volumes.

Serial issue

Although the first edition in book form of *Framley Parsonage* was the three volumes of 1861, its first actual appearance was serially in the *Cornhill Magazine* between 1860 and 1862, and since it was by no means uncommon this practice needs some explanation. From about 1830 publishers had found a huge new market for cheap monthly magazines that included part of a new work of fiction in each issue, and they vied with each other to sign up prominent authors for their productions. Many famous novels started in this way, although they would usually be revised and polished for publication in three-volume book form.

The *Cornhill Magazine* (founded in 1860) was one of the most important of these new magazines and was edited by Thackeray. It had contributions from Thackeray himself and from Tennyson and Ruskin among others and it was illustrated by the rising artists of the day. A close rival was *Macmillan's Magazine*, which serialised Kingsley's *The Water Babies* and Henry James's *Portrait of a Lady*.

Most collectors are content to collect the novels of a favourite author in convenient book form, and usually there is no priority of issue, since the book would usually be ready for publication just

'Nicholas Nickleby' in the original nineteen one shilling monthly parts, 1838-9. The same title bound up in book form without the wrappers and advertisements can be seen on page 62.

before the serialisation was concluded. However, the serial issue does often preserve the author's original thoughts, and collecting them is, in the words of Graham Pollard, 'important and difficult [and] to the real collector this is recommendation enough'.

Parts issue

Parts issue was originally a clever scheme to sell the coloured plates of a popular illustrator such as Rowlandson, whose famous *Dr Syntax's Tours* appeared in parts, each with a couple of coloured plates and a portion of text by a professional hack, one William Combe. That the emphasis in this form of publication was shifted from the artist to the author is due largely to the genius of Charles Dickens (1812-70).

The first of Dickens's novels issued in this way was *The Pickwick Papers*. There were twenty monthly parts in nineteen issues (the last being a double number) and in each the reader received two engraved plates, some thirty pages of text and an assortment of advertisements at the front and the rear, all contained within blue printed wrappers for one shilling. Its

An inserted slip from part 6 of 'Edwin Drood', showing the options offered by a London binder to anyone who wanted to bind up his parts.

18, *Gracechurch Street*,
London, E.C.

September 1870

The present number completes the volume

of *Mystery of Edwin Drood*

I shall be happy to bind it for you in the undermentioned styles, at the prices stated.

Yours respectfully,

JAS. GILBERT.

Publisher's cloth case	2/.
Half plain calf	2/9
Half calf, Half extra	3/6
Half morocco, cloth sides	4/-

success was phenomenal and was repeated for almost all of Dickens's novels, including *Nicholas Nickleby* (1838-9), *Martin Chuzzlewit* (1843-4), *Dombey and Son* (1846-8) and *David Copperfield* (1849-50).

When starting a novel in parts issue the author usually had little idea how the story would end, and to this day the conclusion to *Edwin Drood* is unknown, since Dickens died when only six parts had been issued in 1870 and left no plan (he probably had none) for the continuation of the novel.

These novels may still be found in all the original parts (often lacking some of the inserted advertisements) but more often the wrappers and advertisements have been removed the body, as it were, of each of the parts collected and bound in a contemporary half morocco or calf. Since the parts were crudely stitched with three needlemarks along the inside edge of the leaf, it is easy to tell if a volume has been bound from the parts by opening it and looking for these stab marks. The publishers would also keep back or reprint some sheets of the complete text and subsequently bind them up to sell separately to those people who had missed the parts. Since these do not comprise the separate parts bound up, they are referred to as the *first edition in book form*.

Dickens also experimented with issuing his books as three-deckers – *Oliver Twist* (1836) and *Great Expectations* (1861) – and also in serial form, for example *Hard Times* in *Household Words* from April to August 1854.

5. Travel and topographical books

Writings on foreign parts for the curious at home are much older than printing but were usually, like the *Travels of John Mandeville*, mid fourteenth century, closer to fiction than fact. The true travel book, in which the author describes his journey and the things and places he has seen, does, however, have an early precedent; this is Bernard von Breyndenbach's *Peregrinationes in Terram Sanctam* (1486), which deals largely with the pilgrimage route to the Holy Land and contains seven accurate panoramas of famous cities. Wild exaggeration of places, people and customs, with monsters and fabulous plants, is, however, the norm in travel books over the following centuries and is either charming or infuriating according to one's taste.

Most people who collect travel and topographical books are inspired by a particular place or country that they know well because they live there, have holidayed there or just because it sounds exciting, but it is worth remembering that there is much competition for second-hand and antiquarian books on certain parts of the world, the Middle East for example, and much less for others, Scandinavia perhaps, or even India. Pirates, explorers, diplomats, soldiers, archaeologists, anthropologists and businessmen have all been authors of the sea voyages, memoirs, military campaigns, excavations, studies in folklore and economy in foreign parts which we may lump together as 'travel books'. Apart from the enormous interest of these first-hand accounts of places, people and things perhaps not described before in English, travel books are usually of great charm for their illustrations: in the eighteenth century with copperplates or aquatints; in the nineteenth with wood or steel engravings or even tipped-in photographs; and in the twentieth with reproductions of photographs or watercolours. Many have maps and plans, perhaps folding and tucked into a pocket in the endpapers, giving valuable information on routes, stopping-off places and cities of the age. Books with illustrations will almost always have a list of plates and maps just after the contents leaf and this should always be checked for completeness.

The Grand Tour

At first, from the sixteenth to mid eighteenth centuries, the Grand Tour was a leisurely two or three year trip through

Europe with Italy as destination undertaken by sons of the aristocracy to improve their languages, social manners and knowledge of antiquities. Later it became possible for, and popular with, the rich middle classes, often now with an eye on good business contacts. The first surviving account is Sir Kenelm Digby's *Journal of a Voyage into the Mediterranean* of 1628, but first published from the manuscript by the Camden Society in 1868. The first guidebook proper is probably James Howell's *Instructiones for Forreigne Travel*, 1642, based on his twenty years abroad. It gives an excellent picture of travelling conditions prevailing at the time of John Milton's famous tour through France to Italy. Some famous literary names have left accounts of their Continental travels: Joseph Addison, *Remarks on Several Parts of Italy* (1705); Tobias Smollett, *Travels through France and Italy* (1766), which was parodied by Sterne in his *Sentimental Journey* (1768), as well as Boswell and Gibbon.

Guidebooks

The most famous are those started in 1832 by Karl Baedeker of Coblenz with a guide to the Rhine. He died in 1859 and the business expanded rapidly under his son Fritz, who moved the business to Leipzig in 1873, by which time almost every country and region in Europe and western Asia had its guidebook, in German, English and French. Distinctive in their flexible red cloth bindings, Baedekers have many accurate folding maps and plans on thin paper. From 1875 onwards they were wire-stapled on an imported American machine. This was revolutionary at the time but has not proved a good idea as the staples rust and damage the paper and the books fall apart.

The similar *Murray's Hand-Books* were started by John Murray III in 1836 with his own on Holland. He also wrote those for France, southern Germany and Switzerland. The series, with more than twenty-five titles, was reprinted, revised and enlarged up to the close of the century. The most famous is Richard Ford's anonymously published *Hand-Book for Travellers in Spain* (two volumes, 1845), which is a classic. He prepared a more manageable version, *Gatherings from Spain,* in 1846 and second and third editions of the original book in 1847 and 1855.

Later Continental travel

The aid to travel provided by these guidebooks, together with the ease of the arranged tours organised from the 1840s onwards by firms such as Thomas Cook (who published their own guidebooks issued free to customers), led to a greater demand for travel books as souvenirs for those who had travelled, as stimuli for those who planned to and as a comfort for the arm-chair traveller. The most attractive are the de luxe volumes published from the 1830s that were illustrated with steel-engraved plates and often in fancy bindings of cloth or leather. Two examples are William Beattie's *Switzerland* (1836) and Miss [Julia] Pardoe's *Beauties of the Bosphorus* (1836), both illustrated by W. H. Bartlett, who also wrote and illustrated his own *Forty Days in the Desert* [1849] and *The Nile Boat* (1850). Also of interest are the ten Jennings Landscape Annuals, which start with *The Tourist in Italy* of 1830 and finish with *Portugal* in 1839. The four volumes of this collection dedicated to Spain (1835-8) are illustrated by David Roberts, famous for his impe-rial folio volumes, full of lithograph plates, on the Holy Land and Egypt. The Landscape Annuals each have twenty-one steel-engraved plates and ten wood engravings as vignettes and are still to be found in their publisher's pretty roan binding. It will be noticed that Spain, Turkey and Egypt, once very much on the periphery of European travel, were by this time, if still exotic, well established as tourist destinations.

Miss Pardoe's work of 1836 was proof that women were now allowed to travel in male company, but this is a very early example of a travel book by a woman and it was not until the 1860s that they became more common; in the 1870s and 1880s they seem to outnumber those by men (Queen Victoria had removed many taboos with her *Leaves from the Journal of Our Life in the Highlands* [1868]). As is to be expected given the age, they are rather shallow (probably mostly deliberately) on art, architecture and geography, but full of delightful accounts of day-to-day bumps, bugs and banter and with very little of the snobbish superiority of men's writing about foreigners.

One of the most popular and attractive collections of the twentieth century was A. & C. Black's Popular Series of Colour Books ('Black's Colour Books'). They were started in 1901 as vehicles for watercolourists and are all illustrated with colour plates, handsomely bound and (from the new series of 1922) with coloured dustjackets. Mortimer Menpes was one of their most prolific author-artists, and one of his most attractive titles is *Japan* of 1901. Another contributor was J. Fullylove with *The Holy Land* (1902) and *Greece* (1906). The same firm published more than sixty topographical and county titles in their Black's Home Guide Books series by Sutton Palmer, A. R. Hope Moncrieff and others.

We have seen how in the eighteenth century some grand literary figures turned their hands to travel writing. In the nineteenth century we have Charles Dickens with *American Notes* (1842) and *Pictures from Italy* (1846); and in the twentieth century Hilaire Belloc with *The Path to Rome* (1902); Rebecca West, with a book on Yugoslavia, *Black Lamb and Grey Falcon* (1944); Sacheverell Sitwell, *Spain* (1950); Rose Macaulay, *The Pleasure of Ruins* (1953); Gerald Brenan, *South from Granada* (1957); and Lawrence Durrell, *The Greek Islands* (1978). But professional travel writers are not wanting either: Eric Newby, *A Short Walk in the Hindu Kush* (1958) and *Slowly down the Ganges*; Bruce Chatwin, whose first book was *In Patagonia* (1978) and whose last was *The Song Lines* (1987); and Patrick Leigh Fermor, whose books include *The Traveller's Tree* (1950) and *A Time to Keep Silence* (1953).

Voyages of discovery

Of travel overseas nothing can compare with the European discovery by Columbus of the New World in 1492, the announcement of which was made public in a two-page printed 'letter' addressed to Ferdinand and Isabella of Spain, printed in Barcelona in 1493. Only one copy survives. The name 'America' had first been used in 1507, but the famous map-maker Mercator was the first, in 1538, to sanction its use for the whole of the continental land mass (unfairly since the name celebrates Amerigo Vespucci, rather than Columbus).

Other voyages of exploration followed, the most celebrated being Magellan's circumnavigation completed in 1522 and described in *Epistola de Adimatile et Novissima Hispanorum* (1523), an account by one of the eighteen survivors of the 265 man crew. Drake's similar feat of 1577 to 1580 was not published until 1628 in *The World Encompassed*, which includes an engraved world map. Many of the great voyages of the period were not separately published and survive only in the collected editions of such worthy editors as Theodore De Bry and Richard Hakluyt.

De Bry's *Collectiones Perigrinationes* in twenty-five parts (Latin Edition), 1590-1634, are better known as the *Grands et Petits Voyages* merely because one series, describing travels to the Americas, is a little taller in size than the second, which describes Africa and the Far East. The collection, highly desirable and rare, is profusely illustrated with very fine engravings and maps, usually engraved by the De Bry family themselves.

Similar but a little less monumental is Hakluyt's *Principall Navigations* (1589), which collects the epic voyages of only the English nation and is a prime source for information on Drake, Raleigh, Hawkins, Cabot and many others. An enlarged edition in three parts was published from 1598 to 1600. When Hakluyt died his manuscripts and notes were acquired by Samuel Purchas, who collected the unpublished material with some additions of his own in *Purchas His Pilgrimes* (four volumes, 1625).

Other collections of contemporary voyages were made by John Churchill (enlarged edition, eight volumes, 1752), John Pinkerton (seventeen volumes, 1808-14) and Robert Kerr (eighteen volumes, 1811-24).

These old books are scarce and expensive, and the Hakluyt Society was founded in 1846 to reprint these texts and hundreds more. Nowadays they are published with scholarly introductions and notes.

Captain Cook

Of the great explorations of the eighteenth century the most important were those of Captain James Cook (1728-79), a labourer's son from Whitby, who, more than any other, made people aware of the vastness of the Pacific Ocean and of the diversity of its island populations. His three voyages in the *Endeavour*, *Resolution* and *Discovery* were described in official accounts prepared for the Admiralty from the original journals and published in eight quarto volumes. They are: *An Account of the Voyages ... for Making Discoveries in the Southern Hemisphere* (prepared by John Hawkesworth), three volumes, 1773; *A Voyage towards the South Pole and round the World*, two volumes, 1777; and *A Voyage to the Pacific Ocean*, three volumes, with a further atlas volume of plates, 1784. This last was posthumously published, Cook having been murdered by natives in Hawaii. These publications were preceded by several unofficial accounts written by other crew members (who were supposed to give up their journals to the Admiralty), notably one Ellis, who received 50 guineas for his *Authentic Narrative of a Voyage* (two volumes, 1782), which gives further details of Cook's death. The complete *Journals* of Cook, which are much more extensive than the published accounts, were edited by Beaglehole and published in seven volumes from 1968 to 1974.

To finish this section on voyages of discovery, we should mention space travel, surely a most profitable subject for a collector of modest means. Official NASA reports and publications are not difficult to find, nor is Neil Armstrong's *First on the Moon* of 1970.

African exploration

The earliest information to reach Europe about the mysterious interior of Africa came from Arab slave traders or from the slaves themselves. One such ex-slave was Leo Africanus, whose *The History and Description of Africa*, published first in Italian in 1556 and translated into English in 1600, was a standard reference work for two centuries, inaccurate though it is. Mere idle curiosity about Africa was replaced by a determination to explore the continent systematically and publish accurate accounts when the Association for Promoting the Discovery of the Interior of Africa was founded in 1788, and three pioneering Scotsmen led the way.

James Bruce (1730-94) sailed up the Nile to Aswan, explored parts of Nubia and then calmly traced the sources of the Blue Nile in Abyssinia, publishing his account in 1790 in five handsome quarto volumes illustrated with copperplates. At almost the same time Mungo Park (1771-1806) was exploring West Africa by tracing the course of the great Niger river, and incidentally introducing his readers to Timbuktu. He returned to Britain and published his best-selling *Travels in the Interior of Districts of Africa* in 1799, two further editions being called for in the same year, but he could not settle in Scotland and was murdered by natives on the Niger in 1806. His *Journal,* found with his body only in 1812, was published in 1815.

The most famous name in African exploration is that of David Livingstone (1813-73), a member of the London Missionary Society, who first went to South Africa in 1840. Between 1841 and 1856 he travelled widely in the interior, including stretches along the Zambesi river, and he discovered Lake Ngami and the Victoria Falls. He returned to England to publish his account in *Missionary Travels and Researches in South Africa* (1857), a marvellous volume which became a bestseller (twelve thousand copies of the first edition were printed). It is full of interesting wood engravings (including a startling tsetse fly on the titlepage), two folding maps (one ingeniously tucked

First edition of Livingstone's account of his historic travels in Africa.

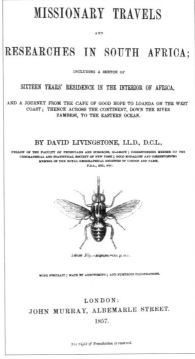

MISSIONARY TRAVELS

AND

RESEARCHES IN SOUTH AFRICA;

INCLUDING A SKETCH OF

SIXTEEN YEARS' RESIDENCE IN THE INTERIOR OF AFRICA,

AND A JOURNEY FROM THE CAPE OF GOOD HOPE TO LOANDA ON THE WEST COAST; THENCE ACROSS THE CONTINENT, DOWN THE RIVER ZAMBESI, TO THE EASTERN OCEAN.

BY DAVID LIVINGSTONE, LL.D., D.C.L.,

FELLOW OF THE FACULTY OF PHYSICIANS AND SURGEONS, GLASGOW; CORRESPONDING MEMBER OF THE GEOGRAPHICAL AND STATISTICAL SOCIETY OF NEW YORK; GOLD MEDALLIST AND CORRESPONDING MEMBER OF THE ROYAL GEOGRAPHICAL SOCIETIES OF LONDON AND PARIS, F.R.A., ETC, ETC.

Tsetse Fig.—magnum, etc. p. 01.

WITH PORTRAIT; MAPS BY ARROWSMITH; AND NUMEROUS ILLUSTRATIONS.

LONDON:
JOHN MURRAY, ALBEMARLE STREET.
1857.

The right of Translation is reserved.

into a pocket in the inside of the rear cover) and a fine steel-engraved portrait of the author with a facsimile of his signature below. In the first issue the folding frontispiece of the Victoria Falls and two other plates are chromolithographs, and these were replaced with cheaper wood engravings in the later issues.

Livingstone returned to Africa and continued his explorations in central Africa, publishing *The Zambesi and Its Tributaries* in 1865. By now his was a household name in Britain and when no word was heard from him for some time it was feared that he might have died in the jungle. The *New York Herald*, shrewdly aware of the interest, sent its ace reporter, Henry M. Stanley (later knighted), to find and rescue the great explorer. This Stanley did, finding Livingstone in weak condition but unwilling to leave Africa, and Stanley returned alone and published his famous *How I Found Livingstone* in 1872. This volume has an attractive gilt pictorial block on the upper cover showing the first meeting of the two men, with the immortal words 'Dr Livingstone I presume?'

Livingstone did die soon afterwards and his body was buried in Westminster Abbey amid a blaze of interest, ensuring a large sale for his *Last Journals* (two volumes, 1874), which includes a moving account of his last moments obtained verbatim from his two African helpers.

Stanley was by no means a spent force and he later travelled widely in the Congo, describing his adventures in *Through the Dark Continent* (1878). His famous *In Darkest Africa* (two volumes, 1890) describes his rather bizarre efforts to rescue the pro-British Emin Pasha, governor of Equatoria, who had been cut off from British forces by the Mahdi revolution in the Sudan. This book was very successful and is not uncommon, being often found with the attractive pictorial binding in fresh condition. There was also a large-paper de luxe issue, which Stanley signed.

One of the most interesting episodes in the history of African exploration is the race to find the source of the Nile, 'the problem of all ages'. Arab traders described the river as originating deep in the interior beyond the Mountains of the Moon. The first to tackle this problem was a Victorian of heroic stature, Sir Richard Burton (1821-90), who described his early travels in Abyssinia in *First Footsteps in East Africa* (1856), and whose other books on Africa include *A Mission to Gelele, King of Dahome* (two volumes, 1864), which contains an account of the army of Amazons in which Burton in typical fashion sets the record straight about the legendary women soldiers, and *Gorilla Land* (1875).

Under the auspices of the Royal Geographical Society, and with John Hanning Speke as his second in command, Burton explored the northern end of Lake Nyasa and discovered Lake Tanganyika, but, falling desperately ill, he allowed Speke to explore further north on his own and Speke discovered the southern end of Lake Victoria. Burton was disinclined (wrongly) to believe Speke's conviction that this was the source reservoir of the Nile and they quarrelled, whereupon Speke returned to England and immodestly aired his views in *Blackwood's Magazine* in 1859. He was answered by Burton in *The Lake Regions of Equatorial Africa* (two volumes, 1860).

To satisfy himself of the accuracy of his judgement, Speke set out again in 1860, this time with J. A. Grant, and thoroughly explored Lake Victoria, finding that the Nile did indeed flow out of it at the Rippon Falls. He triumphantly published the facts in *Journal of the Discovery of the Nile* (1863). Grant and Speke were subsequently the first Europeans to cross equatorial Africa, a feat described in Grant's book *A Walk across Africa* (1864).

On the way home the explorers had met the remarkable Sir Samuel Baker, travelling up the Nile with his wife. Already a veteran explorer of the Blue Nile in Abyssinia, Baker had determined to do more work on the Nile sources and received much useful information from Speke. He found a third lake to the west of Victoria in 1864 and showed that the waters of this lake flowed from the Murchison Falls to join the Nile waters. He published *Albert Nyanza* in two volumes in 1866, this being the name he gave the third lake.

Apart from these tales of exploration, the public avidly followed the colonial campaigns and wars such as the Ashanti, 1873 and 1896, the Zulu, 1879, and the Boer, 1899-1902, firstly in periodicals like *The Illustrated London News*. Odd yearly bound volumes are often come across and are full of first-hand accounts by the combatants, rushed to London along with drawings or photographs to be copied by teams of wood-engravers. Some of these wood engravings are folded in the periodical and can be as large as 16 by 24 inches (40 by 60 cm). They are made up of several blocks cut by different hands for speed; the thin lines where the blocks were joined can often be seen. Later would come the full account in a book.

Despite the end of the golden age of African exploration and the peace after the Boer War, many interesting and original books on Africa continued to be written by such authors as Harry Johnston (discoverer of the okapi), Mary Kingsley and Charles Eliot. Some of these have become famous, like Karen Blixen's *Out of Africa* (1937). Official or company propaganda for would-be colonists in the form of illustrated books and pamphlets (coffee, tea or peaches) should be watched

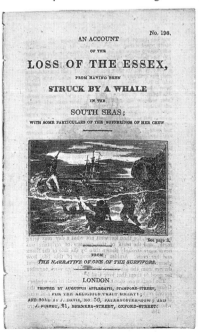

A twelve-page edifying pamphlet published for the Religious Tract Society and sold for '4s per 100' to retailers. That thousands were printed to be given away or sold cheaply is shown by the wood engraving, which has split from heavy use. This copy has been 'disbound', that is broken up from a bound volume.

out for. They contain a wealth of information and are rarely expensive.

Topography

The study of local history and topography is an Elizabethan invention. The first county history was William Lambarde's *Perambulations in Kent* (1576), which was to have been the first of a series until the author learned that William Camden was engaged on a similar project. The latter's famous *Britannia* was first published in 1586 and much reprinted, each successive edition containing more and improved county maps: 1607 with Saxton's, 1695 with Morden's and 1789 with Cary's.

Perhaps the most interesting attribute of topographical books is the wealth of engraved views and plans which they contain, and this is already evident in the seventeenth century in such works as Sir William Dugdale's *History of St Paul's Cathedral* (1658), with its superb engravings by Wenceslaus Holler, and David Loggan's *Oxonia* and *Cantabrigia* of 1675 and 1688. These books pioneered the 'bird's-eye view' with prospects of the colleges, a technique brilliantly used again by John Kip in *Britannia Illustrata* (four volumes, 1736) to show country houses with their parks.

A school of writers appeared in the eighteenth century to cater for the appetites of a public increasingly interested in touring for its own sake and anxious not to miss any of the delights of the landscape or 'picturesque' beauty. Among these Thomas Pennant, Samuel Ireland and William Gilpin (satirised as *Dr Syntax* by Rowlandson) were the most prolific and their elegant topographical volumes are usually illustrated with copperplate engravings or the newly discovered aquatint process.

The period from the late eighteenth century to the mid nineteenth was the great age of the amateur and there was a boom in local and county histories, a classic example being Gilbert White's *A Natural History of Selborne* (1789), which has a place in this chapter because of his careful descriptions of the topography and history of the parish. Usually county histories are unpretentious volumes, although this could not be said of Blore's *History of Rutland* [1811], which is about 3 feet (914 mm) high! Locally printed and illustrated and issued in small numbers, they are consequently very often scarce although they are rarely expensive. A great deal of their charm lies in the very wide range of topics which they usually manage to cover, with a typical volume, *Brighthelmstone* by J. Erredge, published in

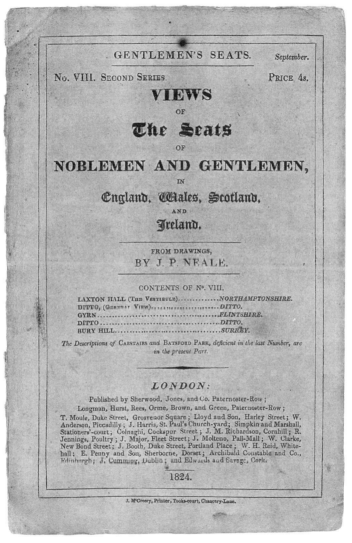

GENTLEMEN'S SEATS.   *September.*

No. VIII. SECOND SERIES.   PRICE 4s.

VIEWS

OF

The Seats

OF

NOBLEMEN AND GENTLEMEN,

IN

England, Wales, Scotland,

AND

Ireland.

FROM DRAWINGS,

BY J. P. NEALE.

CONTENTS OF Nº VIII.

The Descriptions of CARSTAIRS *and* BATSFORD PARK, *deficient in the last Number, are in the present Part.*

LONDON:

Published by Sherwood, Jones, and Co. Paternoster-Row;
Longman, Hurst, Rees, Orme, Brown, and Green, Paternoster-Row;
T. Moule, Duke Street, Grosvenor Square; Lloyd and Son, Harley Street; W. Anderson, Piccadilly; J. Harris, St. Paul's Church-yard; Simpkin and Marshall, Stationers'-court; Colnaghi, Cockspur Street; J. M. Richardson, Cornhill; R. Jennings, Poultry; J. Major, Fleet Street; J. Molteno, Pall-Mall; W. Clarke, New Bond Street; J. Booth, Duke Street, Portland Place; W. H. Reid, White-hall; E. Penny and Son, Sherborne, Dorset; Archibald Constable and Co., Edinburgh; J. Cumming, Dublin; and Edwards and Savage, Cork.

1824.

J. McCreery, Printer, Tooks-court, Chancery-Lane.

An amusingly titled, finely illustrated (with steel engravings) topographical book published in parts. Notice the great number of participating publishers and booksellers who shared the cost and profits.

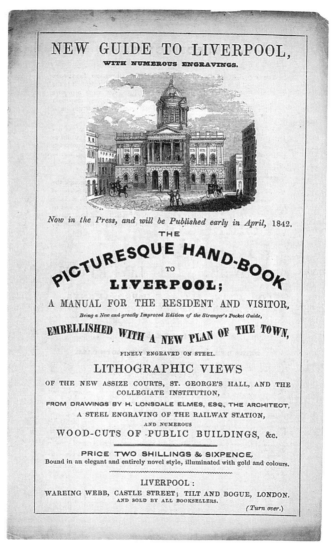

NEW GUIDE TO LIVERPOOL,
WITH NUMEROUS ENGRAVINGS.

Now in the Press, and will be Published early in April, 1842.

THE

PICTURESQUE HAND-BOOK
TO
LIVERPOOL;

A MANUAL FOR THE RESIDENT AND VISITOR,

Being a New and greatly Improved Edition of the Stranger's Pocket Guide,

EMBELLISHED WITH A NEW PLAN OF THE TOWN,

FINELY ENGRAVED ON STEEL.

LITHOGRAPHIC VIEWS

OF THE NEW ASSIZE COURTS, ST. GEORGE'S HALL, AND THE
COLLEGIATE INSTITUTION,

FROM DRAWINGS BY H. LONSDALE ELMES, ESQ., THE ARCHITECT,

A STEEL ENGRAVING OF THE RAILWAY STATION,

AND NUMEROUS

WOOD-CUTS OF PUBLIC BUILDINGS, &c.

PRICE TWO SHILLINGS & SIXPENCE,
Bound in an elegant and entirely novel style, illuminated with gold and colours.

LIVERPOOL :
WAREING WEBB, CASTLE STREET; TILT AND BOGUE, LONDON.
AND SOLD BY ALL BOOKSELLERS.

(*Turn over.*)

An advertisement for a typical guidebook of the period, illustrated with wood and steel engravings and lithographs and all in a fancy binding.

Brighton in 1867, indulging not only in a history of the town but in a description of the climate, ornithology, botany and geology of its vicinity.

County libraries may be a good source for information on local and county histories. There was a time when county librarians made special efforts to collect and preserve all they could on the subject or to pamper potential donors, but nowadays they are just as likely to have sold off the best books.

Many excellent topographical books have been published in the twentieth century, most notably the monumental *Victoria County Histories*, which originated in Queen Victoria's reign, and the discerning collector will soon single out for his special attention such series as the *Batsford British Heritage* of the 1930s (including *English Abbeys* and *The English Country House*) and Nikolaus Pevsner's *Buildings of England*, which started with *Cornwall* in 1951 and reached number 35 *Worcestershire* in 1968. The earlier titles were in paperback.

The famous *Shell Guides* were edited by John Betjeman and begin with his own *Cornwall* in 1934. The artist John Piper wrote and illustrated number 11, *Oxon*, in 1938 (changed to *Oxfordshire* for the new edition of 1953). As Shell were the promoters rather than the publishers, the titlepages bear various imprints, such as Architectural Press, Batsford and Faber, and are often not dated.

Chiang Yee's *The Silent Traveller in Lakeland* (1937) was the first of several *Silent Traveller* books which see the country through the eyes of a contemplative foreigner. *London* came out in 1938, *The Yorkshire Dales* in 1941, *Oxford* in 1944, *Edinburgh* in 1948 and *Dublin* in 1953, with two foreign titles, *New York* and *Paris*, added in 1950 and 1956. Chiang was an artist and calligrapher (he wrote an excellent book on Chinese calligraphy) and illustrated all of these books, and their dustjackets, with his own charming watercolours and line drawings in a very Chinese style.

6. Children's books

A subject with immediate appeal and plenty of nostalgia, collecting children's books is now very popular and the early works and first editions of the classics are by no means readily available or cheap. The term *children's books* is to be preferred to *juvenilia,* which more properly describes books written by children, such as the famous *Young Visiters* by Daisy Ashford, written when the author was nine and published with a preface by J. M. Barrie in 1919, or Jane Austen's *Love and Friendship,* first published from the manuscript only in 1922.

Although the history of children's books can be traced back to the German *Kunstund Lehrbüchlein* of 1580, which contains woodcuts by Jost Ammann, the first publisher in England to concentrate on this lucrative market appears to have been Thomas Boreman, who issued some eleven volumes for children from 1736, a good proportion of them dealing with giants.

Boreman's efforts, however, were soon eclipsed by the activities of John Newberry (1713-67) and his son Francis (1743-1818), whose attractive little publications dating from 1744, usually with crude woodcuts and bound in pretty Dutch floral boards or in the 'vellum manner' (quarter green vellum), are widely celebrated. Their most famous books are *Mother Goose's Tales,* known only from the seventh edition of 1777 (which includes first appearances of, amongst others, 'Hush-a-bye Baby', 'Hey Diddle Diddle' and 'Jack and Jill') and *Goody Two Shoes* (one copy only of the first edition of 1765 survives), which was probably written by the great Oliver Goldsmith. He worked for Newberry from 1762 to 1767 and Newberry was the publisher of his *Citizen of the World* (1762) and *She Stoops to Conquer* (1773).

The first published volume solely of nursery rhymes was *Tommy Thumb's Pretty Song Book* (?1744), in which appear 'Baa Baa Black Sheep', 'Sing a Song of Sixpence' and 'Oranges and Lemons' amongst others. Two other early books of nursery rhymes, *Gammer Gurton's Garland* (1784) (with 'Goosey Goosey Gander') and *Songs for the Nursery* (1805) (with 'Little Miss Muffet') were both published by rivals of Newberry.

Fairy stories

The first fairy stories for children were possibly invented by Charles Perrault but more probably by his son Pierre, whose

Histoires ou Contes du Temps Passé was published in 1697 and translated into English in 1727 by R. Samber. All the tales are narrated by Mother Goose and they include such favourites as 'Cinderella', 'Puss in Boots' and 'Sleeping Beauty'. Another great collection was gathered from country folk tales by the brothers Jakob and Wilhelm Grimm, and the first English edition of *German Popular Stories* appeared in 1823-6. The two volumes are illustrated with twenty-four etched plates by George Cruikshank, his first important book commission. Much later, in 1909, an attractive edition was illustrated with coloured plates by Arthur Rackham. Hans Andersen's *Wonderful Stories for Children* was first published in England, translated from the Danish, in 1846.

The nineteenth century

During the nineteenth century attention was turned to the children's book as never before, and a number of authors of adult books as well as professional men in other fields, including a landscape artist (Lear) and a mathematician (Carroll), achieved outstanding success with their incursions into the field. The earliest of these, apart from Charles and Mary Lamb (both professional authors, whose twenty *Tales from Shakespeare* was published in two volumes in 1807), was William Roscoe (1753-1831), an eminent historian who wrote *The Butterfly's Ball and the Grasshopper's Feast*, published first in 1807 with six engravings. It was immediately and hugely popular but, although revived by William Plomer in 1973 with brilliant illustrations by Alan Aldridge, it has not remained a favourite among children.

A Christmas Carol (1843) by Charles Dickens (1812-70) was similarly successful and, with its pretty gilt-tooled cloth binding and four hand-coloured plates by John Leech, is one of the most charming books of the century. Six thousand copies were sold in the two weeks before Christmas but Dickens was not pleased to find that he had made only £137 out of publication. The first issue of the first edition should have the title printed in red and blue and 'Stave I' rather than 'Stave One' at the opening of the text. Dickens's *A Child's History of England* (three volumes, 1852-4) is also scarce in good original condition.

Charles Kingsley (1819-75) published his *Water Babies* in 1863 with illustrations by J. Noel Paton, and some copies have a leaf before the text with a rather strong poem entitled 'L'Envoi'. This was suppressed by Kingsley during printing and copies with it are scarce. Even the great John Ruskin (1819-1900) tried his hand at entertaining children with a delightful story, *The King of the Golden River,* published in 1857 with illustrations by Richard (Dicky) Doyle. A new edition was published in 1934 with illustrations by Rackham.

Edward Lear and Lewis Carroll

Edward Lear (1812-88) did not invent the limerick but, with his immortal *Book of Nonsense* by Derrydown Derry, published by himself in a small edition in 1846, he made the form peculiarly his own. Lear was a master of lithography (having published his folio volume on parrots in 1830 in that medium) and in the first edition the delightful illustrations are lithographed with the verses below on some seventy-eight leaves, although the collation is erratic. But for the new enlarged edition, which he likewise paid for himself, he commissioned Dalziel to make cheaper wood engravings from the drawings.

This new edition, still anonymous, was issued for Lear by Routledge in an edition of one thousand copies in 1862, after which Lear sold them the copyright for the tiny sum of £125. Some of his best-loved verses (and he never stopped penning them) appeared in much later works: 'The Owl and the Pussy Cat' in *Nonsense Songs* (1871) (with *More Nonsense Pictures* following in 1872), and both 'The Quangle-Wangle' and 'The Yonghy-Bonghy Bo' in *Laughable Lyrics* (1877).

Charles Lutwidge Dodgson (1832-98) was a deacon and lecturer in mathematics at Oxford, where he published pieces on such varied topics as vivisection and lawn tennis. He first used the pseudonym 'Lewis Carroll' to sign an article called 'Solitude' which appeared in a monthly magazine, *The Train,* for March 1856. It is well known that Carroll related the original of his most famous story to the three Liddell girls, Alice, Lorina and Edith, on a boat trip from Oxford to Godstow in July 1862 and, on being begged by Alice to write it all down, spent the whole night setting out what he could remember of *Alice's Adventures in Wonderland.*

Carroll expanded this first version and arranged for publication by Macmillan, but at his own expense, and illustrations by Sir John Tenniel were included. The volume was ready in June 1865 but Carroll was not satisfied with the quality of printing and ordered the entire edition to be returned to him (although eighteen copies are known to have survived). The volume was reprinted, now with the date 1866 on the titlepage, and although

The Mad Hatter's Tea Party from 'Alice's Adventures in Wonderland' (1865).

this is technically the second edition it is usually termed the first [published] edition, since the 1865 edition was not strictly published. It is a handsome volume, printed on good quality paper and bound in crimson cloth with gilt blocking and edges. The manuscript of the first version was published in facsimile in 1885, and the manuscript itself, after some years abroad, was presented to the British Museum in 1948 by a group of Americans to thank 'a noble people who held Hitler at bay'.

The sequel, *Through the Looking Glass and What Alice Found There*, was published in similar format in 1871, again with illustrations by Tenniel, who caricatured himself as the White Knight, although that character represents the author. Two other books, *Sylvie and Bruno* (1889) and *Sylvie and Bruno Concluded* (1893), were less successful than Carroll's *Hunting of the Snark* (1876), which has striking illustrations by Henry Holiday. This is not an uncommon book since the first edition consisted of ten thousand copies, and some are known with dustjackets, early examples of that inconvenient article. Noteworthy editions of *Alice* have been illustrated by Harry Rountree, Charles Robinson, Arthur Rackham, Millicent Sowerby and Mervyn Peake.

Boys' books

Boys' books may be said to originate with Frederick Marryat (1792-1848), who published *Midshipman Easy* in 1836 and *Masterman Ready* in 1842, each in three volumes and both based on his own experiences of seafaring. *Masterman Ready* deals with life on a desert island, always a popular subject, from Daniel Defoe's *Robinson Crusoe* (1719) to William Golding's *Lord of the Flies* (1954). Thomas Hughes's anonymous *Tom Brown's Schooldays* (1857), R. M. Ballantyne's *Coral Island* (1858) and *The Young Fur Traders* (1856), W. H. Kingston's *Peter the Whaler* (1857) and Sir Henry Rider Haggard's *King Solomon's Mines* (1886), *She* (1887) and *Allan Quatermain* (1887) are examples in the classic mould.

The work of G. A. Henty (1832-1902) is now widely collected as representing the apogee of the boys' book with its ripping good story, lively illustration and, perhaps most strikingly, its cloth cover usually bearing a coloured pictorial block. These pictorial bindings do indeed look impressive when in fine condition. Henty's output was prodigious and his success dates from the 1880s when he became editor of the influential *Union Jack Magazine* for boys. He produced over ninety titles, including *Under Drake's Flag* (1883), *Beric the Briton* (1893) and *With Kitchener in the Sudan* (1903).

Robert Louis Stevenson (1850-94) first published his greatest story in *Young Folks Magazine* between October 1881 and January 1882 as *The Sea Cook* by Captain North, but as *Treasure Island* (1883) it has become one of the most successful adventure stories ever written. Like *King Solomon's Mines*, it has a folding facsimile of an old map bound in as a frontispiece. *Kidnapped* was published in 1886, with the sequel *Catriona* following in 1893, and another immortal adventure story, *The Black Arrow,* in 1888. Stevenson also wrote the much loved *Child's Garden of Verses* (1885), although thirty-nine of the sixty-four poems were privately printed in *Penny Whistle* in 1883. It was illustrated by Charles Robinson in 1895.

Angela Brazil

Angela Brazil (1868-1947) was the doyenne of the girls' book and almost all of her fifty or so titles are set in girls' schools. Her first sets the pattern: *The Third Class at Miss Kayes* (1909). This was followed by *Bosom Friends, A Seaside Story* in 1910 (undated). The Edwardian titles are bound in attractive pictorial cloth over thick boards, like Henty's books.

An illustration from Kate Greenaway's 'Marigold Garden' (1888).

Kate Greenaway and Randolph Caldecott

Greenaway (1846-1901) and Caldecott (1846-86) are the most famous children's illustrators of the latter part of the nineteenth century, and they shared an imaginative publisher, George Routledge, and a brilliant printer, Edmund Evans.

Their books are printed throughout (including the covers, be they boards or wrappers) by a process perfected by Evans in which each illustration was printed in colour using a sequence of superimposed wood blocks (flesh, green, yellow and so on). Both sprang to popularity in the same year, 1878: Greenaway with *Under the Window* (undated), a book of her own illustrated verse, and Caldecott with the first two of his sixteen 'toy books', *John Gilpin* and *The House that Jack Built* (again undated). They were both prolific illustrators, Greenaway genteelly Regency, elegant and pretty, Caldecott lively, sporty and humorous. Among Greenaway's books are Browning's *Pied*

51

Piper [1881], *The Language of Flowers* (1884), *Marigold Garden* [1888] and a series of annuals, 1883 to 1897, as well as some magazine work; and among Caldecott's, Irving's *Old Christmas* (1875), *Aesop's Fables* [1883], *The Great Panjandrum* [1885], and a host of periodical illustration.

Almost all of their books are undated and were reprinted well into the twentieth century, but it is important to obtain early impressions if possible. A Routledge imprint on the titlepage is proof of a nineteenth-century printing as Frederick Warne (Beatrix Potter's publisher) took over the titles at the turn of the century. With Caldecott, a reference to the list of 'toy books' on the back cover will tell you if it is early (obviously if you have a copy of *The Mad Dog* [1880] and the list includes *Mrs Mary Blaize* [1885], yours is post-1885). There is a useful checklist in Muir (see Bibliography, where a bibliography of Greenaway is also listed).

Beatrix Potter

Like Greenaway with her own books of verse, Beatrix Potter (1866-1943) devised a formula in which the illustrations and a simple text are of equal importance. Her first books, *The Tale of Peter Rabbit* and *The Tailor of Gloucester*, were both privately printed in editions of two hundred and fifty and five hundred copies in 1901 and 1902, the first published editions being issued in 1902 (undated) and 1903. Other now famous titles followed almost every year, including *Benjamin Bunny* in 1904, *Mrs Tiggy Winkle* in 1905, *Jemima Puddle-Duck* in 1908, *Flopsy Bunnies* in 1909 and *Mr Tod* in 1912.

All but *Peter Rabbit* [1902] are clearly dated on the titlepages of the first editions. The volumes were all issued at one shilling in boards but many titles were also available in cloth gilt for sixpence extra, and two titles, *The Tailor of Gloucester* and *Squirrel Nutkin,* both 1903, were also issued in a delightful de luxe chintz which was made at Beatrix Potter's grandfather's works at Manchester.

Peter Pan

The endearing boy hero of Never-Never Land has a somewhat complex bibliographical history. He was first written about by Sir James M. Barrie (1860-1937) in chapters 13 to 18 of *The Little White Bird* (1902), after which the parts concerning him were gathered together with slight alterations and published in 1906 as *Peter Pan in Kensington Gardens*, which was beautifully illustrated with fifty coloured plates by Arthur

(Top left) *'Winnie the Pooh' by A. A. Milne (1926): the second volume in the quartet, this fine copy has the dustjacket designed by Shepard.* (Top right and bottom left) Two first editions in the original boards of Beatrix Potter tales (1904 and 1909). (Bottom right) *Henry Williamson's 'Tarka the Otter' (1927): a nice copy with dustjacket designed by Hester Sainsbury.*

Rackham. Meanwhile Barrie had been turning the story into a play and this was performed in 1904. This drama was turned back into prose for *Peter Pan and Wendy*, illustrated by F. D. Bedford [1911] (undated, but later impressions record the fact on the verso of the titlepage), and the play complete was published as *Peter Pan or the Boy Who Never Grew Up* in 1928 in the uniform edition of Barrie's works. A memorable edition was also illustrated by Mabel Lucie Attwell in 1921.

Pooh books and others to date

Probably the most famous children's books of the twentieth century are the four Pooh books by A. A. Milne (1882-1956). *When We Were Very Young* (1924) is much the scarcest of the four although all are difficult to find with dustjackets; the others are *Winnie the Pooh* (1926), *Now We Are Six* (1927) and *The House at Pooh Corner* (1928). All are inimitably illustrated by Ernest Shepard, who is also remembered for his illustrated edition of Kenneth Grahame's *Wind in the Willows* (1931), the first edition of which had been published in 1908 but with only one rather feeble illustration by Graham Robertson.

Rudyard Kipling (1865-1936), who started his writing career

One of Ernest Shepard's illustrations from 'Winnie the Pooh' (1926).

as a journalist in India, wrote several classics for children, *The Jungle Book* (1894) and *The Second Jungle Book* (1895) being the most famous, although *Kim* (1901) is considered by some to be his best work. *Just So Stories* was illustrated by Kipling himself (his father had illustrated *The Jungle Books*) and was published in quarto format with pictorial covers. *Puck of Pook's Hill* followed in 1906. The swastika found with an elephant and lotus flower stamped on some of Kipling's books is the ancient Sanskrit sign for well-being.

The twentieth century's most prolific children's author (and the first to appear in paperback) was Enid Blyton (1897-1968), whose 'Noddy Library' started in 1949 with *Noddy Goes to Toyland* and finished with number 23, *Noddy and the Tootles,* in 1962. All were issued with dustjackets. Among her more than four hundred published books are three well-known series: fourteen 'Famous Five' books, beginning with *Five on a Treasure Island* in 1942; twelve 'The Mystery of...' stories starting with *The Mystery of the Burnt Cottage* in 1943; and the six titles of which *The Secret Seven* (1949), was the first.

Blyton also translated Jean de Brunhoff's *Histoire de Babar* as *Tales of Babar* (1941) and *The Babar Story Book* (1942), although the first in English was *Babar and the Little Elephant* (1934), followed by *Babar's Travels* (1935) and *Babar the King* in 1936. They are all in folio format and attractively printed lithographically in colours.

Another prolific author was 'Richmal Crompton' (Richmal Crompton Lamburn, 1890-1969), who published no less than thirty-eight 'William' books between 1922 (*Just William* and *More William*; both undated) and 1968 (*William the Superman*). Although Crompton attempted to keep her stories topical, e.g. *William and the Space Animal* (1956) and *William and the Pop Singers* (1965), there is no doubt that William's heyday was the period up to and including the Second World War – *William the Conqueror* [1926], *William the Gangster* [1934], *William the Dictator* [1938], *William and the Evacuees* [1940]. It will be seen from the square brackets that these early titles are not dated on the titlepage but new impressions and editions are recorded as such on the verso. The well-known image of scruffy William with his grubby knees is due to Thomas Henry Fisher, who illustrated all but the last four books. He also worked for *BOP* (see below) and was, incidentally, responsible for the sailor trademark for Players tobacco.

Walt Disney (1901-66) produced the first of his Mickey

A typical illustration by Thomas Henry Fisher from the first 'William' book, 'Just William', 1922.

"SHE'S A SOPPY OLD LUNY!" DORITA REMARKED SWEETLY.

Mouse animated cartoons in 1928 and did not at first see the value of a book tie-in. The first book to contain Mickey Mouse drawings by the Walt Disney Studios was *The Mickey Mouse Story Book* by Bobette Biro, which came out two years later and was not published by Disney. The success of the book was not lost on Disney, however, and from *The Mickey Mouse Annual* (1930, and continued) onwards he controlled all aspects of his creations. *The Adventures of Mickey Mouse* came out in 1931, with *Donald Duck's Book* in 1936, *Pluto's Playtime* in 1937 and *Snow White, Sketches for the Film* in 1938. None of these books is dated but since they were generally dropped or changed after a year or two at most you can be sure, if you find one, you have at least got an early printing. Disney also started a series of annuals for the Christmas market: *Walt Disney's Happy Annual* in 1937, *The Donald Duck Annual* and *The Snow White Annual* (both in 1938), a tradition that continues to this day.

Arthur Ransome (1884-1967), a great nature lover and writer and ace reporter during the Russian Revolution, is now famous for his 'Swallows and Amazons' books which tell of the adventures of the Walker and Blackett families on the Norfolk Broads and in the Lake District. The first, which gives its name to the series, was published unillustrated in 1930. The second edition came out simultaneously with *Swallowdale* in 1931, both illustrated by Clifford Web. The remaining titles are illustrated by the author himself.

The seven 'Chronicles of Narnia' by C. S. Lewis (1898-1963), an Oxford don and religious writer, begin with *The Lion, the Witch and the Wardrobe* and *Prince Caspian* in 1950 and 1951 and end with *The Last Battle* in 1956. All are illustrated by Pauline Baynes, who also illustrated four books, including *Farmer Giles of Ham* (1946), but not the Hobbit books, for Lewis's friend and contemporary at Oxford, J. R. Tolkien (1892-1973). *The Hobbit* (1937) introduced readers to Tolkien's invented mythical world of Middle-Earth and the saga was continued with *The Fellowship of the Ring* (1954), *The Two Towers* (1954) and *The Return of the Ring* (1955).

The 'Railway Series' by the Reverend Wilbert Awdry (1911-97) started in 1942 with *The Three Railway Engines, Thomas the Tank Engine* following in 1945. By 1970, with steam engines already a thing of the past, twenty-five titles had appeared, all in distinctive oblong 16mo format. The first ten titles are very attractively illustrated by C. R. Dalby. All have a series number, but the first editions of numbers 1-4 do not bear a number as these were given them retrospectively.

Watership Down (1973) was Richard Adams's first book and, in circumstances similar to those pertaining to the creation of Alice, was expanded from a tale told to keep his two daughters amused during a car journey. It only became hugely successful when issued by Puffin Books (the famous children's branch of Penguin, run for many years by Kay Webb) in 1973 and this edition, in paperback with a cover by Pauline Baynes, is probably scarcer than the first, of which two and a half thousand were printed. A new edition, illustrated by John Lawrence, was published in 1976, one of the most handsome books of the decade. Adams's other books for children include *The Ship's Cat* (1976), illustrated by Alan Aldridge, *Tyger Voyage* (1977), illustrated by Nicola Bayley (a collected illustrator whose first book, *Nursery Rhymes*, was published in 1975) and *The Iron Wolf* (1980).

Periodicals and comics

Periodicals for children first appeared at the beginning of the nineteenth century. Because they are sometimes found bound up or issued in yearly volumes by the publisher, some will be mentioned here. The most famous of all is *The Boy's Own Paper,* the first volume of which came out in 1879 (with *The Girl's Own Paper* following in 1880); it continued until the 1930s. *BOP,* as it was familiarly known, also published its own subject books, all of them, like *The Boy's Own Paper Cycling Handbook* [1932], eminently practical. Another Victorian favourite was *The Boy's Own Magazine,* edited by S. O. Beeton (husband of Mrs Beeton of cookbook fame) and first published in volume form in 1855-62 (the first as *The Boy's Own Volume*), with another collection 1870-4. More public-school sporty was *The Captain* (1899-1924), the yearly volumes issued in typical stamped pictorial bindings.

In the first decades of the twentieth century perhaps the best loved boys' paper was *The Magnet,* with its tales of Greyfriars School and its five famous pupils, including Billy Bunter. The stories were mostly written by Charles Hamilton (1876-1961), calling himself 'Frank Richards'. *The Magnet Library* started in 1908 and the first annual seems to be *The Greyfriars Holiday Annual* for 1929, but the 'Bunter' books proper begin in 1947 with *Billy Bunter of Greyfriars School*, followed by *Billy Bunter Barring-Out* in 1948 and *Billy Bunter in Brazil* in 1949. There are at least forty more, published unfailingly every year to the author's death. Up to 1955 they are illustrated by R. J. Macdonald, and thereafter by C. H. Chapman.

What we now know as comics, that is periodicals consisting of collections of cartoon strips, boomed in popularity after the Second World War. Bound-up copies of the actual comics are very scarce because they have almost always been treated as ephemera, but all comic publishers (and D. C. Thompson is the best known) appreciated the market for a special compilation volume just before Christmas and brought out their various annuals. They are usually in attractive coloured boards that carry the date of the year ahead and even those from the 1950s and 1960s already have a period flavour. Three that spring to mind are *The Hotspur Book for Boys* [1934 onwards], *The Beano* (the first annual, called *The Magic Beano Book*, came out in 1948) and *The Eagle Annual* [1951 onwards], now much appreciated for its Dan Dare strip by Don Harley and Bruce Cornwall.

Rupert Bear started as a comic strip in the *Daily Express* in 1920. The drawing was by Mary Tourtel and the story-line by her husband, H. B. Tourtel, and the first book of cartoons from the paper, *The Adventure of the Little Lost Bear,* appeared undated in 1921, followed by *The Little Bear and the Fairy Child* [1922], also undated. These two are in 16mo format but the forty-six volumes of 'The Little Bear Library', published between 1928 and 1936, are in 8vo; the more familiar 4to format was started in 1929 with 'The Monster Rupert' series. The character was taken over in 1936 by Alfred E. Bestall and he was responsible for the *The Rupert Story Book* [1938], *Rupert Again* [1940] and all of the annuals up to 1973.

Novelty books

Children's books with some sort of novelty feature have a history of at least two centuries. In the eighteenth century conventional story books were sold alongside 'panoramas', long fold-outs with a coloured picture telling a story and set within card covers, and 'harlequin' books, with four or more flaps lifting vertically or horizontally to change a picture. These were the simple forerunners of the 'movable' books which contained an elaborate system of flaps to be lifted in various directions to produce a scene or play with a picture. These are known from as early as the middle of the nineteenth century, and the invention is attributed to Dean & Son, who published more of them than anyone. By the 1880s and 1890s they had become somewhat more common as well as colourful, being printed in gaudy chromolithography, mostly in Bavaria, where skill was abundant and cheap. One German publisher who produced books for the British market in these decades was Ernest Nister of Nuremberg and London, who commissioned texts from British authors. His books, movable or not, are characterised by highly chromolithographed covers and content with a surfeit of sentimentality. It was he who invented (or re-invented) the stand-up book, which we now call pop-ups. The earliest were worked manually by pulling on a ribbon, but later the effect was produced by the leverage on the hinges when the book was opened. A typical example in the Osborne collection is *The Children's Holiday Coach* [1895], with a poem on the front which is illustrated by opening the covers to reveal the stand-up picture inside. The firm of Raphael Tuck is another famous name in pop-ups, publishing these books from the early years of the twentieth century up to the 1950s. Pop-up books have always been complicated and costly to produce and have never been very common. When found they are usually in poor condition, with queens' heads and rabbits' ears missing. They were revived in the 1970s, but with an adult audience in mind.

From the 1860s the publisher Darton issued books printed on paper-coated linen in an attempt to give them a longer life in the nursery, and he called them 'indestructibles'. They are rarely found, however, in good condition. The first books printed directly on cloth were the Dean's Rag Books, which started around 1905; many are not dated, but they usually have a series number.

The recent books which have a pressure pad set into the cover which emits a battery-produced sound (perhaps a chirruping cricket or a police siren) might be compared to the squeaky books, which date from at least the 1920s, where a fat tummy or delicate hand is pressed to produce the sound.

Conclusion

With children's books the illustrations are often an important part of the whole (indeed, as we have seen, not a few are by the authors themselves) and the artists have always been mentioned in this book. Many of them worked for various authors and publishers, and collecting their work is just as worthwhile as collecting authors.

There is no space in this brief survey to include more than a few of the famous children's books of the twentieth century, but there follows a list of some first appearances of other favourites. Square brackets mean that there is no date on the titlepage. The note 'and x more' means that there are more books about the same character or characters; many authors wrote other, quite different books and some (like Johns with 'Gimlet'), even had other series running in parallel:

Nesbit, Edith. *The Story of the Treasure Seekers* (1899), *The Railway Children* (1906).

Baden-Powell, Robert, Lord. *Scouting for Boys, a Handbook* [1908] with the 'Complete Edition' (1909), *Girl Guiding, a Handbook* (1918).

Lofting, Hugh. *The Story of Dr Dolittle* (1920) and eleven more, all illustrated by the author.

Barker, Cicely. *The Book of Flower Fairies* [1927] with nine more 'Flower Fairy' books, but now dated, to 1955; illustrated by the author.

Uttley, Alison. *The Squirrel, the Hare and the Little Grey Rabbit* (1929) and twenty-seven more 'Little Grey Rabbit' books, all illustrated by Margaret Tempest; *The Adventures of Sam Pig* (1940), illustrated by Francis Gower, and seven more 'Sam Pig' books.

Johns, Captain W. E. The first 'Biggles' adventure, *The Cruise of the Condor* [1933], appears in the 'Ace Series of Flying Stories'; two more follow in the same series, and then *The Black Peril* [1935] with about forty subsequent stories, from 1943 illustrated by L. L. 'Studio' Stead.

Travers, Pamela. *Mary Poppins* (1934) and three more, all illustrated by Mary Shepard, E. H. Shepard's daughter.

Buckeridge, Anthony. *Jennings Goes to School* (1950) and sixteen more. Later titles illustrated by D. C. Mays.

Norton, Mary. *The Borrowers* (1952) and three more, illustrated by Diana Stanley.

Ryan, John. *Captain Pugwash* (1957) and many more to date, illustrated by the author.

Smith, Dodie. *The Hundred and One Dalmatians* (1956), illustrated by Janet and Anne Grahame-Johnstone; *I Capture the Castle* (1959).

Bond, Michael. *A Bear Called Paddington* (1958) and many more to date, illustrated by Peggy Fortnum.

Garfield, Leon. *Jack Holborn* [1964], illustrated by Anthony Maitland, and other historical novels.

7. Bindings

Once the manuscript roll of remotest antiquity had been super-seded by the codex (gatherings of leaves sewn together), it became necessary to protect it above and below with some form of tough covering. The earliest surviving bookbindings, from fourth-century Egypt, had already solved the problem by using a natural goatskin cover, sometimes decorated, with flaps to protect the fore-edges, and other slightly later bindings also found along the Nile valley consist of plain wooden covers with leather spines and joints. Generally all bookbinding has been done with one of four materials: vellum (or parchment), tanned leather, paper (boards or wrappers) and cloth, and these are separately treated below.

Vellum

Vellum is the skin of a young calf or lamb prepared for use by polishing with alum (parchment is the tougher skin of the

Some binding styles: (left to right) original boards with the edges uncut; half morocco with marbled paper sides and edges; full morocco, with decorative gilt spine in panels and with gilt edges; vellum.

matured sheep) and was used for heavy-duty binding, school-books, sermons and the like up to the eighteenth century. It has been found to be extremely durable. For heavier books, wooden covers of oak or beech (from which last the word 'book' derives) were used. These were then covered with vellum or parchment, often decorated with blind tooling, sometimes with a central pictorial panel representing a scene from scripture or the classics, and finished with brass bosses and clasps.

Because vellum or parchment (at least in Britain) is more expensive to prepare than leather, is easily soiled and is not a good surface for decorative tooling (and many parchment bindings have the title lettered on the spine, not tooled), its use had all but disappeared by the eighteenth century, when it was revived as an affectation by the celebrated firm of Edwards of Halifax (*floruit* 1755-1820) for use on volumes of elegantly printed verse which they sold in their London shop. James Edwards, son of the firm's founder, invented a method of treating part of the vellum to be used for covering a book to make it transparent, and, this done, he had a view or portrait painted on the underside, so that when the book was bound the painting would show clearly beneath the covers but still be fully protected. The same inventive firm also revived the art of fore-edge painting, particularly the variety which, not visible when the volume is shut tight, may only be viewed when the edges are furled open in a slanting position.

Apart from this Regency vogue, the use of vellum for binding is rare, exceptions being the special, deliberately archaic decorative bindings produced for the private presses such as Kelmscott and Doves and where plain vellum in the manner of Elizabethan trade (printer's own) bindings was also used. Cedric Chivers of Bath revived, in the 1890s, James Edwards's idea of painted bindings where the decoration is painted on the underside of translucent vellum. These he called 'Vellucent bindings'.

Leather

Leather for binding is obtained by soaking the raw animal skin (calf or morocco, which is goatskin) in an infusion of oak bark, a process called tanning. Leather bindings (and indeed vellum and cloth bindings) are usually *full*, that is both covers and the spine are in leather; but other styles do occur, most notably *half binding*, where the spine and the corners only are covered in leather, the space between being filled out with cheaper cloth or marbled paper, and *quarter*, where just the

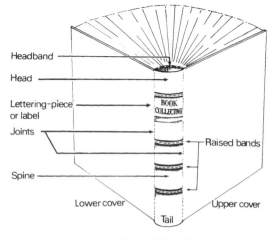

Headband

Head

Lettering-piece
or label

Joints

Spine

Lower cover

Raised bands

Upper cover

Tail

BOOK
COLLECTING

FULLY BOUND VOLUME

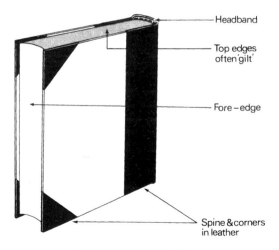

Headband

Top edges
often 'gilt'

Fore-edge

Spine & corners
in leather

HALF BOUND VOLUME

Leather bindings.

spine is leather-covered. This is slightly different to American usage, which describes Britain's half bindings as *three-quarter.*

Decorated bindings

The earliest surviving European decorated leather binding covers the remarkably pristine Northumbrian *Stonyhurst Gospel*, a small manuscript of the Gospel of St John bound in dyed goatskin, which is moulded over interlacing cords on each cover. It was completed and bound towards the end of the seventh century. For many years it lay in the coffin of St Cuthbert, but it was removed under threat from the Vikings and is now on long loan to the British Library. This sort of 'sculptured' binding would not be seen again until the papier-mâché covers of Victorian times (see below) and the designer bookbindings of the present day.

In general, book covers were decorated by 'tooling', which is done by first marking out the overall design layout in 'blind', then placing gold-leaf on the surface of the leather and pressing on it a heated tool which has an individual design on its face, like a punch. The gold adheres to the leather according to the design on the tool, which may be dots, circles, a flower, a bird or arabesques and the like and can be repeated all over the surface as the binder wishes. In addition the binder has a collection of wheels: a simple one, rather like a pastry-cutter, when run over the surface produces a line, called a *fillet*; wider ones, like cotton reels, when run around the edges of the covers or in the centre forming a rectangle, produce a 'roll-tooled border or panel'. He will also have decorative blocks to fill a corner or centre-piece (perhaps a coat of arms). The binder does not have to use gold-leaf: if the heated tool is pressed directly on to the leather it leaves an impression in 'blind', as we have already seen with early parchment bindings over boards. Blind tooling had a vogue in Puritan England when Bibles and prayer books were covered in black morocco and 'tooled all over' in blind. These are the so-called 'sombre bindings'. The idea was revived in Victorian times, again largely for religious works. It is the binder's treatment of the covers (his flair for design, the originality of the tools he uses, or the lack of them) that makes a binding commonplace or a work of art.

Few decorative bindings can rival the commissions executed for the French kings of the sixteenth century, particularly François I and Henri II, who both took a personal interest in the royal library, but the name of one commoner, Jean Grolier

(1479-1565), is at least equally celebrated in this field. He delighted in having the latest scholarly works bound (by at least six different binders, including Claude de Picques) in calf with striking designs of interlacing strapwork, gilt-tooled and hand-painted, and he invented the magnanimous motto '*Jo Grolerii et amicorum*' ('Jean Grolier and friends') to have stamped on his books.

Restoration England

In England the Restoration period was the golden age of bookbinding, when covers were exuberantly filled with flowers, 'drawer-handle' shaped designs, curls, loops and drapes, often arranged around a 'cottage-roof' design. This was where the ubiquitous *panel* was capped with a roof-like triangle, a design which originates with Samuel Mearne (1624-83), the famous binder who worked for Charles II from 1660 to his death. There were other brilliant binders during this period, but although their separate work has been identified very often their names are unknown and they are necessarily referred to by such curious cognomens as 'Spaniel Binder', 'Centre Rectangle Binder', 'Queen's Binder' and so on, which relate to their binding tools, their binding style or their patrons.

The eighteenth century

Roger Payne (1738-97) started his career as a binder in Eton but moved to London in 1766 and was soon working for the greatest book collectors in the land, including Earl Spencer. His bindings are characterised by his use of straight-grained morocco, with the lettering tooled in several (rather than one or two) panels on the spine with dotted backgrounds, and of panelled sides with floral swags at the corners and wide gilt-tooled borders, but he is equally celebrated for his verbose and expensive bills and for his hopeless inebriety. Henry Walther, John Baumgarten and Christian Kalthoeber are among a number of German craftsmen who came to England with the Hanoverian monarchy and produced excellent work in the classical style with motifs borrowed from ancient Greece and Rome; these designs would be roll-tooled or continually repeated in gilt to form decorative borders.

The Victorian period

Vigorous and inventive, the Victorian age produced some bookbindings of remarkable originality. H. N. Humphries produced gothic papier-mâché bindings to imitate carved ebony and they were used to cover his own illuminated volumes. They were made by applying the papier-mâché to a metal frame and moulding it to the required design; eight such bindings were produced, from *Parables of Our Lord* (1847) to *Sentiments and Similes of Shakespeare* (1857), the most striking of the group, which has a terracotta-like plaquette in the centre of each cover. Equally impressive is the huge *Victoria Psalter* published in 1864, illuminated by Owen Jones, who also designed the binding of moulded (or *relievo*) calf over stout boards, the effect being of two carved panels in pearwood by Grinling Gibbons.

Other Victorian binding conceits include covers made to imitate malachite or copper ore, as in Longfellow's *Tales of a Wayside Inn* (1867), and the use of a small piece of timber from a locality connected with a famous author to provide covers for an edition of his poems; thus an edition of Scott's *Poems* of 1853 has covers of wood from timber at Abbotsford. Other wooden bindings (usually of plane), with pictorial transfers, or even photographs, under a highly varnished surface, are generi-

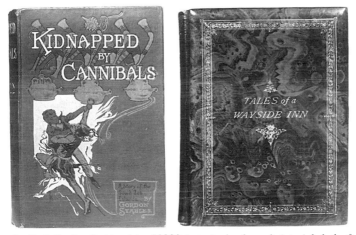

(Left) *A Gordon Stables title of 1900, in typical coloured pictorial cloth of the period, to sell at 5 shillings and published by Blackie, a famous name in boys' book publishing.* (Right) *An ingenious Victorian gift binding of heavy glazed boards with green marbling underneath imitating malachite (copper ore). This volume of Longfellow's verse (1867) is one of a small number produced for Bell & Daldy.*

A Mauchline ware binding of wooden boards with pictorial transfers, covering 'Ballad Minstrelsy of Scotland', Glasgow, 1871. The portrait is of Sir Walter Scott.

cally known as Mauchline ware bindings after the Scottish village where most of them were made from the middle of the nineteenth century onwards.

Great trade craft binders of the age include Charles Lewis, Francis Bedford, Sangorski and Sutcliffe (known especially for their jewelled bindings) and Rivière (commissioned by Sotheran at the turn of the century to produce the Cosway bindings, which have a hand-painted miniature on ivory set into the covers).

Armorial bindings

Armorial bindings are those which bear a coat of arms or an armorial device on the covers, an impressive way of declaring provenance before bookplates become commonplace. Volumes bearing the royal arms, spectacular and interesting though they can be, are not necessarily from the monarch's own library. It has always been possible for a loyal subject or parish to order a Bible or prayer book already bound with the royal arms and other more subtle clues must be assessed before a royal provenance can be firmly established.

Armorial bindings became very much less common after Regency times but were revived later in the nineteenth century for use as school prizes (the earliest the present author has noticed is 1840). The prize volume was bound in calf or morocco with a usually splendid armorial school stamp gilt-blocked on the upper cover. These prize bindings are still to be met with at reasonable prices and would form an interesting collection.

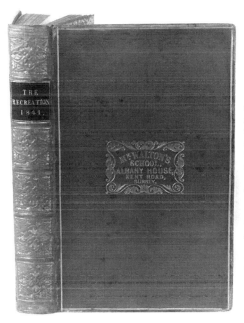

An early example of a prize binding in full calf, with a gilt panelled spine (and incidentally with plates on art paper). On the front pastedown is a label with the pupil's name, 'praiseworthy and zealous... in prosecuting his studies'. The Recreation, MDCCCXLI, a gift book for young readers, Edinburgh, John Menzies [1840, late in the year].

(Left) *'Psalms of David' (1862), an Edmund Evans wood-engraved book with a superb cloth binding tooled in gilt and blind by an unknown designer.* (Right) *A remarkable papier-maché binding on an H. N. Humphries illustrated book, 'Records of the Black Prince' (1849).*

Paper (boards or wrappers)

Books in paper wrappers are found sporadically throughout the centuries from incunable times onwards. They may be plain or overprinted with a design or simple title, but from the seventeenth century they are very often of coloured or marbled paper, brought from Holland or France. When paper-covered cardboard is used the book is said to be 'in boards', and this is the form in which the great majority of books were sold from the eighteenth century onwards. The outer paper is usually grey, with a printed title label stuck on the spine. This cheap but fragile binding style lasted right up to the 1840s, for twenty years being used contemporaneously with cloth, and even after this date continued in the coloured pictorial board bindings known as 'yellowbacks' (see chapter 10). In general practice, however, purchasers of serious books would take them to a binder for a more permanent leather covering, hence the relative scarcity of books in boards. After the Second World War some book clubs started binding their books in boards and by the mid 1950s many publishers (ever alert to a good cost-cutting idea) had also reverted to the practice and they are once again the standard trade binding in England (the 'hardback') – but now with dustjackets.

For modern paperbacks, see chapter 10, 'Popular editions and series'.

An early, and battered, example of a cloth binding with the title gold-blocked on the spine, that is to say, impressed from a block and not separate letters. The earliest gold-blocking is thought to date from 1826. 'Spain, Yesterday and Today', London, Darton & Harvey (a famous name in children's books), 1834.

Cloth bindings

Binding in cloth has a long history. Surviving examples show that Queen Elizabeth I particularly liked velvet and in early Stuart times there was a fashion for binding Bibles and prayer books in embroidered cloth, the so-called 'needlework' bindings. It is possible that some were produced by workshops but more likely that the embroidery was done by the lady of the house and then handed to the binder. At any rate they were all one-offs, and even the calico-bound schoolbooks of the eight-eenth century, still sometimes to be found, were commissioned by schools, presumably in class-size numbers, for their own use as a cheap and hard-wearing alternative to leather or boards and cannot be considered trade bindings (that is, a binding ordered by the publisher for the whole edition). The first recorded use of cloth in a trade binding is on a set of Horace in the Diamond Classics series published by William Pickering in 1820. It seems so obvious to us now, but the novelty took time to catch on and publishers hedged their bets, sometimes using boards and sometimes cloth, for a long time afterwards. The earliest cloth-bound books had a printed paper title label stuck on to the spine but within a few years it was realised that cloth could be lettered in gilt as easily as leather and by the late 1820s, in another step forward, simple blocking was being

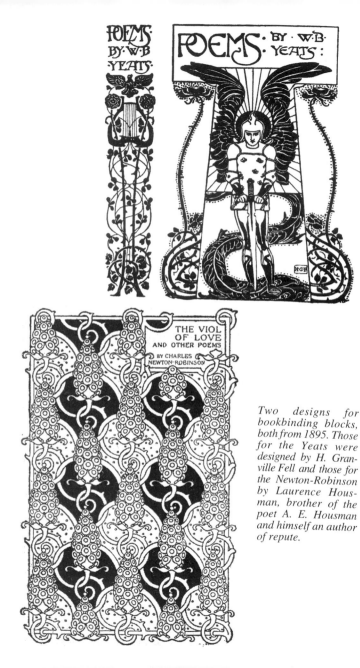

Two designs for bookbinding blocks, both from 1895. Those for the Yeats were designed by H. Granville Fell and those for the Newton-Robinson by Laurence Housman, brother of the poet A. E. Housman and himself an author of repute.

used. *Blocking* is stamping the whole design on the covers with one or more ready-cut metal blocks rather than building it up with individual tools. The technique was in full stride by the mid 1830s, becoming ever more exuberant until it filled spine and covers, sometimes in gilt, sometimes in blind, and the Keepsakes and Ladies' Annuals of the period to the late 1840s, still cheap, are excellent examples of the best on offer at the time. Blocking was to be in regular use by all publishers for the next hundred years.

The 1860s are usually taken to mark a high point in book production and much original thought and talent went into design, including the covers. (See the illustration of the *Psalms of David,* 1862, on page 70, the covers and spine blocked in gilt

An exotic colour-blocked binding on a book from 1910. The sixteen colour half-tone plates inside are 'mounted at large'.

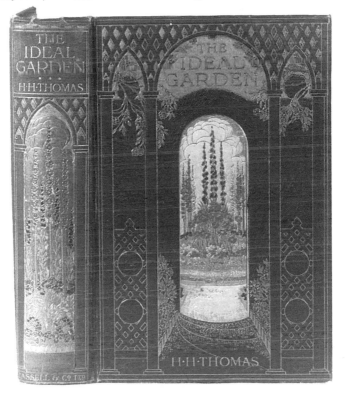

and blind to a design by an unknown artist.) If there is something special about 1860s books, that is not to say that there was a subsequent falling off, as the covers of books in the Cranford series (1875-91) show (see chapter 10). Sometimes the covers are blocked with designs by well-known artists. Those on the *Alice* books for example (1865 and 1872) are after drawings in the text by Tenniel, and D. G. Rossetti's *Poems* of 1870 is blocked with a lovely, almost Art Nouveau design by the painter-poet himself, while John Ruskin's *Studies in Both Arts* (1895) has a lovely cover by Edward Burne-Jones.

A notable binding of the 1890s is on *Silver Points* by John Gray (1891), which has pointed leaves in formation attached to a curtain of vertical waving lines. It was designed by Charles Ricketts (1866-1931), already an excellent book illustrator and founder of the Vale Press. He also designed several bindings for Oscar Wilde's books, including the important *House of Pomegranates* (1891) and *Poems* (1892), and two bindings for Thomas Hardy, *A Group of Noble Dames* and *Tess of the D'Urbervilles* (both 1891). The two book cover designs illustrated on page 72, both from 1895 and typical of the day, are by H. Granville Fell and the author Laurence Housman.

Cover blocking in colour was introduced for boys' books from the 1880s, but by the 1890s it was used also for adult books with popular appeal, such as Nansen's *Farthest North* (second edition, two volumes, 1898). The tradition continued through Edwardian times with such works as Winston Churchill's *My African Journey* (1908), which had a typical pictorial binding showing the author in front of a shot rhinoceros, and with such excellent series as the A. & C. Black travel books, which were published up to the Second World War.

Fore-edge painting: a volume with the edges furled open to reveal a fore-edge painting, which disappears when the volume is closed.

Dustjackets

It is still rather a new idea to consider the dustjacket as an integral part of the book and to demand its presence. From the earliest days up to the first decades of the twentieth century they were considered mere protective coverings, meant to be discarded once the book had been taken home, and were uniformly dull, and for this reason dustjackets up to this time are rarely found. The earliest known survives on a copy of Heath's *Keepsake* for 1833. It is a plain buff-coloured paper with the title overprinted in red and protects a fragile watered-silk binding. Another nineteenth-century survivor, in one copy only, is on the first book edition of *Edwin Drood* (1870).

While a publisher was spending money on blocking the covers of his books he may have given them a dustjacket, but he would certainly have been surprised if it were kept. This attitude lasted well into the twentieth century as curious examples on some of Beatrix Potter's books demonstrate; they are of transparent paper, overprinted certainly, but clearly intended to let the buyer see the attractive picture on the boards below, and once bought would have been discarded.

Two things changed this state of affairs after the First World War: one was the increasing cost of blocking or otherwise decorating the covers when a dustjacket (which was by then *de rigueur*) was much cheaper to print, and the other was the realisation of the enormous potential of the jacket for advertising the book in full colour, including reviewers' comments from advance copies, and for announcing late changes such as the price. Why not switch attention from the cover to the dustjacket?

Modern dustjackets may be roughly classified as either typographical or illustrative. Of the former, such masters as Edward Johnston, David Jones and particularly Stanley Morison have provided designs for jackets. Morison's best work is to be seen on the series of striking dustjackets designed for the publisher Victor Gollancz in the 1930s. Characterised by bold black lettering, sometimes with a little red, often with a paragraph of comment cleverly bringing part of the blurb of the inside fold to the front, they were printed on bright yellow paper. The first of these revolutionary new dustjackets is on *Dialogues and Monologues* by Humbert Wolfe (1931), and one of the most impressive is that for *The Running Footman* by John Owen of the same year.

Illustrated jackets are equally appealing and some of the most celebrated talents have tried their hands at the art: Sir William

Some modern first editions with dustjackets: 'Shardik', Richard Adams (1974); 'Into Battle', Churchill's most famous war speeches (1941); 'Cider with Rosie', Laurie Lee (1959); 'The Go-Between', L. P. Hartley (1953); 'The Heart of the Matter', Graham Greene (1948); 'Black Girl', Bernard Shaw (1932), with glassene wrapper; 'Cold Comfort Farm', Stella Gibbons (1932); 'Our Man in Havana', Graham Greene (1958); 'Late Lyrics', Thomas Hardy (1922).

Orpen on Wells's *Mr Blettsworthy* (1928); Vanessa Bell on Virginia Woolf's books from 1921; Robert Gibbings on his own *Over the Reefs* (1948); John Piper on Sadleir's *Forlorn Sunset* (1947); and John Ward on *Cider with Rosie* (1959) and more recently for reprints of Thomas Hardy published by Zodiac.

The colourful dustjackets for the Batsford books of the 1930s, notably the British Heritage Series, are now much in favour. Most of them are by Brian Cook (an alias for the publisher Brian Batsford) and do not have the glazed surface of modern dustjackets. Other notable artists include Rex Whistler, whose jackets cover books by Beverley Nichols and Walter de la Mare; Val Biro, on Evelyn Waugh's *Men at Arms* trilogy and L. P. Hartley's *The Go-Between*; and Philip Gough, who seems to have concentrated on A. L. Rowse with *The Churchills* (three volumes) and his Shakespeare and other Elizabethan books.

It is important to buy copies of modern first editions with dustjackets if possible, but without being fanatical; after all, many copies of a book will inevitably have lost their jackets and there simply may not be enough copies that retain them to go round. First editions with dustjackets will always be scarcer and more expensive; but you may not have the money or want to wait: with or without, you still have the first edition. That said, it certainly would be a shame not to have the dustjacket for *Decline and Fall* by Evelyn Waugh (1928), which was designed by Waugh himself; for Joyce Cary's *Drunken Sailor* (1947), with the blurb written by the author; or for *The French Lieutenant's Woman* by John Fowles (1969), which bears the following statement: 'The author and publisher assure the reader that there are no pagination errors in the final chapter of this story.'

8. Press books

As the name implies, press books or private press books are those printed by hand in the traditional way on the printing press of a private individual, who will himself choose the titles he wants to issue and has nobody but his bank manager to answer to for finance. By having a special fount cut he will ensure a typographical interest and distinctive appearance for the books issued from his press, and these will be printed in strictly limited numbers (usually announced in the colophon or a statement of limitation, which may also be signed by hand) on handmade paper and probably afterwards appropriately bound. Since press books appeal to the connoisseur (not to say the dilettante) rather than to the general public, they are not published in the strict sense but are distributed either by subscrip-

The device of the Strawberry Hill Press showing Walpole's villa at Twickenham.

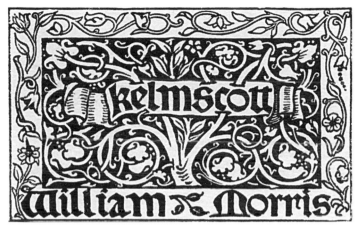

The device of the Kelmscott Press.

tion or through favoured bookshops.

Although the private press has existed since at least 1572, when Archbishop Parker issued *De Antiquitate Britanniae* from his palace at Lambeth, the originator of the press book as we know it is generally held to be Horace Walpole, fourth Earl of Orford (1717-97), whose **Strawberry Hill Press** was founded in 1757 with an attractive edition of new *Odes* by Mr Gray. Named after Walpole's 'gothick' villa at Twickenham, the press issued illustrated works of antiquarian research in which Walpole had a particular interest and also a good selection of contemporary *belles lettres*, some by Walpole himself. The famous William Caslon supplied all of the elegant type used and, in spite of the enormous difficulty Walpole had in keeping his professional printers, he kept the press running for thirty-two years.

The pioneer of the 'do it yourself' press book was C. H. O. Daniel, who began printing in 1845 at the early age of nine in his father's vicarage at Frome. The **Daniel Press** moved to Oxford in 1874 and concentrated on small volumes of elegantly printed poetry, including a good number of first editions by Robert Bridges, and only ceased with Daniel's death in 1919.

Kelmscott Press

After attending in 1888 a lecture on printing by Emery Walker, William Morris (1834-96), a leading figure in the Arts and Crafts movement, was fired with the ambition to apply his

79

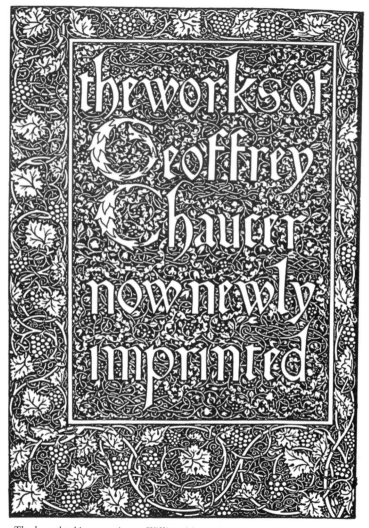

The breathtaking opening to William Morris's Kelmscott Chaucer (1896), printed by Morris himself. Facing this in the original is an equally splendid page with a pictorial woodcut by Burne-Jones.

ideals of traditional craftsmanship and design to the making of books. By showing that the true craftsman could and should be involved in all stages of bookmaking he hoped to effect a reform amongst the somewhat dull professional printers and publishers of his day. Taking as his models the beautiful volumes printed by Jensen, Mentelin and others in the fifteenth century, he designed three types, Golden (1890), Troy (1891) and Chaucer (1892) and, commissioning special handmade papers and inks, he set about learning how to print.

The first book from the Kelmscott Press was Morris's own *The Story of the Glittering Plain*, printed in an edition of two hundred copies in 1891, and, reviving another medieval custom, Morris printed six copies on pure vellum. The press was discontinued after Morris's death, having fifty-three separate works to its credit, all reflecting the founder's passionate love of great literature and in particular his fascination with the sagas and ballads of the middle ages. Most of the Kelmscott books contain Morris's own wood-engraved initials and borders, and many are illustrated with wood engravings after designs by his close friends Sir Edward Burne-Jones and Walter Crane, and these achieve a harmony between printed text and illustration not seen since the Renaissance.

The *magnum opus* of the press is the Kelmscott Chaucer of 1896, illustrated by Burne-Jones and printed in an edition of 425 copies, with some on vellum (including one in the British Library). This magnificent folio volume represents the apogee of the private press movement and is indisputably the most splendid example of English printing.

Other important presses

Morris's books were carefully designed and illustrated, but in spite of his declared intention not to 'dazzle the eye ... or trouble the intellect ... by eccentricity' they are not easily read and the presses which followed Kelmscott tried to counterbalance his archaic influence by eschewing ornament almost entirely. Adopting austere and classical roman typefaces, rather than gothic, such presses as the **Ashendene** (founded by St John Hornby in 1894) and the **Doves** (founded in 1900 by T. J. Cobden-Sanderson, who was also an accomplished and original binder) relied for effect on the overall beauty of the letterforms themselves, allowing only an occasional marginal gloss in red or a calligraphic initial by Edward Johnston. The Doves Press is justly celebrated for the five-volume Bible of

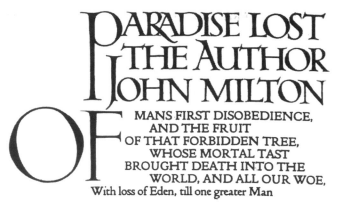

The opening page of the Doves Press 'Paradise Lost' (1902), with lettering by Edward Johnston.

(Above) *A device of the Golden Cockerel Press by John Buckland Wright.*

(Left) *Some typical Nonesuch Press books.*

82

1903-5 with Johnston's initial letter I in Genesis running the length of the page.

The reaction against illustration was not long-lasting, however, and the **Golden Cockerel Press**, founded in 1923, made a speciality of blending the text with original wood engravings. With the artist Robert Gibbings in control from 1924 to 1933, it produced some of the finest illustrated books of the twentieth century, most notably *The Canterbury Tales* of 1929-31 in four volumes and *The Four Gospels* of 1931, both sensuously illustrated by Eric Gill.

The **Nonesuch Press** was set up in 1923 to test Sir Francis Meynell's conviction that machine-made books could and should be as attractive as handmade ones and to show that it was not necessary for a press to be exclusive to be successful. An impressive number of scholarly and handsome editions, some illustrated by Reynolds Stone, McKnight Kauffer, Paul Nash and others, more than proved his point. The 'compendious' series broke new ground with omnibus editions of writers in one stout buckram-bound volume (with de luxe bindings as an alternative); edited by experts such as Geoffrey Keynes, they started with his own *Poetry and Prose of William Blake* in 1927 and eventually included fourteen titles. Titles for children were collected in the Nonesuch Cygnets, which included *Histories Told by Mother Goose* (1925) and *The Book of the Bear* (1926), both bound in attractive patterned paper. A Nonesuch book that is both still easy to find, usually inexpensive, and yet a typical example of the high quality of the press is *The Weekend Book* by Francis and Vera Meynell, which was first published in 1924 and became a bestseller, with new editions over several years.

The best Nonesuch books are the four-volume Bible of 1925, Dante of 1928, Shakespeare in eight volumes of 1929-33 and, most splendid of all, the collected edition of Dickens in twenty-three volumes (1937-8). This was, unusually, printed in a small edition of 877 sets, this being the exact number of original plates and woodblocks illustrating the novels which the press had been able to buy from Dickens's old publishers, and one plate or block was included with each set purchased – an ingenious inducement to tempt subscribers.

Press books, like modern first editions, are particularly susceptible to the irrationalities of collecting fashions, and by concentrating his main attention on some lesser known presses the beginner may quietly and inexpensively acquire an impressive collection exhibiting the main attractions of the genre. Many presses (for example the **Stanbrook Abbey Press**, the oldest surviving press, founded in 1870) issue keepsakes or single printed leaves of poetry and such like as well as the more usual prospectuses, and all of these are examples of the press's work and are collectable.

It is important that press books are carefully handled. Their fragile boards or decorative bindings and handmade papers are easily soiled and any damage greatly reduces the commercial value.

Other important presses are Vale Press (Charles Ricketts, 1894-1903); Eragny Press (Lucien Pissarro, 1894-1914); Essex House Press (C. R. Ashbee, 1898-1910); Shakespeare Head Press (A. H. Bullen, founded 1904 and still active); Hogarth Press (L. and Virginia Woolf, 1917-32); Gregynog Press (G. and M. Davis, 1922-40, now revived); and Cressett Press (D. Cohen, A. Myers, founded 1927).

Lesser known and more recent presses include Caradoc Press (founded 1899), Florence Press (founded 1908), Riccardi Press (founded 1909), Beaumont Press (founded 1917), Hand and Flower Press (founded 1939), Rampant Lions Press (founded 1949), and Whittington Press (founded 1971).

9. Illustrated books

Colour-plate books

The great series of colour-plate books published in the first quarter of the nineteenth century by Rudolph Ackermann and others are among the chief glories of English book production. Ackermann, a German immigrant, pioneered the use of lithography in Britain and developed the technique of printing with aquatint plates so successfully that the finished illustrations look like original watercolours. These illustrations were partially printed in colours and then finished off with superb hand colouring, giving an excellence scarcely equalled since.

Ackermann's most famous books are the *Dr Syntax Tours* (three volumes, 1812, 1820 and 1821), in which rather pedestrian poetry by William Combe is brilliantly illustrated by Thomas Rowlandson. Topography was Ackermann's forte, however, and his stately volumes such as *The Microcosm of London* (three volumes, 1810*), History of St Peter's, Westminster* (two volumes, 1812), *History of the University of Oxford* and *History of the University of Cambridge* (both 1814) are classics. More accessible are the forty-two small volumes from the World in Miniature series of 1821-7, which often occur for sale separately; each volume covers one country, the text illustrated with hand-coloured plates.

Wood engravings

While the sumptuous colour-plate books were directed at the wealthy connoisseur, the wood-engraved illustrations of Thomas Bewick (1753-1828) had far wider appeal. He transformed the crude woodcuts of the broadsides into miniature engravings of exquisite craftsmanship. For his natural history books he developed the formula of depicting the bird or animal described in the text at the head of the page and reserving a space at the foot of the chapter for a little vignette illustrating a sometimes harrowing country scene, and these he called 'tale pieces'. Bewick's best books are *Land Birds* (1797) and *Water Birds* (1804), both much reprinted, but his *Quadrupeds* (1790) and *Aesop's Fables* (1818) are almost equally engaging.

In the competent hands of such craftsmen as the Dalziel family wood engraving became a standard feature of the popular Victorian book, and in particular the gift books of the 1860s are now prized as much for their wood engravings by such artists as Miles Birkett Foster and Daniel Maclise as for their elaborate gilt covers. In the Victorian period many of the finest artists did some book illustration and, although J. M. W. Turner's illustrations (in Rogers's *Poems* of 1834 and elsewhere) are all steel engravings, many artists tried their hand at drawing for wood engraving, including some of the Pre-Raphaelites.

J. E. Millais produced much mediocre work in this field, although some of his illustrations to Trollope are well regarded. His fellow artist in the movement, D. G. Rossetti, was responsible for the first Pre-Raphaelite book illustration, in Allingham's *The Music Master* of 1855. Rossetti also produced some attractive designs for Moxon's edition of Tennyson's works in 1857 and for *Goblin Market* (1862) and *The Prince's Progress* (1866), both by his sister Christina.

After the mid nineteenth century wood engraving began to go into decline, but it was revived by some brilliant artists in the 1920s. The earliest work was commissioned largely by the private presses, most notably the Golden Cockerel, for which Eric Gill did some remarkable illustrations. By the 1930s such

The magpie, an engraving by Thomas Bewick from 'Land Birds' (1797).

One of fifty wood engravings from John Lawrence's hilarious book of Cockney rhyming slang, 'Rabbit and Pork', 1975.

artists as John Farleigh with Shaw's *Adventures of the Black Girl* (1932) and Agnes Miller Parker with Bates's *Through the Woods* (1936) and *Down the River* (1937) had brought the medium to popular attention.

Other important wood engravers of the period are Claire Leighton with *Country Matters* (1937) and *Under the Greenwood Tree* (1940); Robert Gibbings with *Sweet Thames Run Softly* (1940), *Coming Down the Wye* (1942) and *Lovely is the Lee* (1944); and Reynolds Stone with both *A Butler's Recipe Book* (1935) and Bell's *The Open Air* (1946). A revival of coloured wood engraving by printing was gallantly attempted by Gwen Raverat in *The Bird Talisman* (1939) and a few others but proved too laborious for much emulation.

Scraperboard is a similar technique to wood engraving and C. F. Tunnicliffe was an acknowledged master of this medium, illustrated in such books as Bayne's *Call of the Birds* (1942) and *Farm on the Hill* (1949).

Scraperboard illustration by Charles Tunnicliffe from 'Letters from Stockholm', 1947.

Edwardian colour books

By Edwardian times the reproduction of coloured illustrations by photographic methods had reached a state of near perfection and was celebrated by a wealth of publications comparable (though on a less grand scale) with the great Regency colour-plate books. The finest colour books of the period are the productions of Arthur Rackham (1867-1939), whose typical book was in quarto format, printed in large type on thick paper, with the many coloured plates mounted at large on tinted paper, and bound in cloth with pictorial designs on the covers. Among his best books are *Rip Van Winkle* (1905) and *Peter Pan* (1906), while his genius for the grotesque is admirably shown in *The Ingoldsby Legends* (1907), *Grimms' Fairy Tales* (1909) and Edgar Allan Poe's *Tales* (1935).

Edmund Dulac's books were issued in similar format, but the illustrations are somewhat gentler and have an oriental flavour; his *Arabian Nights* appeared in 1907 and *Rubaiyat of Omar Khayyam* in 1909, and both were much reprinted. Both Rackham and Dulac books are expensive, particularly the signed de luxe issues in which they delighted, but some of their contributions in such fine productions as *King Albert's Book* (1914) and *Princess Mary's Gift Book* (1915) are still cheap.

Other artists of the period similarly presented in gift books are Eleanor Fortesque Bricklade, James Thorpe, Maxfield Parrish, Kay Neilson, Mortimer Menpes and Helen Allingham. These last two were published by A. & C. Black, whose excellent colour books have already been mentioned.

Line drawings

Line drawings may be collected from any period, although it takes an artist of rare talent to illustrate his book successfully throughout with just pen strokes. Line illustrations in the text, rather than on separate plates, became successful only with the great advances in photographic reproduction in the 1880s. Hugh Thomson is particularly appreciated for his elegant Regency period studies, and he illustrated many volumes in the Cranford series (see chapter 10) superbly well, including *Days with Sir Roger de Coverley* (1886) and *The Vicar of Wakefield* (1891). Other works include the novels of Jane Austen between 1894 and 1897 and the marvellous *Coaching Days and Coaching Ways* of 1888, by Outram Tristram, which also includes attractive hostelry scenes by Herbert Railton and is still not an expensive book.

Forming a complete contrast is the entertaining work of Phil May, whose Cockney and music hall characters are justly celebrated. His work appeared in *Punch* from 1893 and he joined the staff in 1895, becoming popular enough to have his

A line drawing by Rex Whistler (1905-44), one of the most popular of pre-war artists.

own winter and summer annuals issued up to 1904.

E. H. New, a prolific artist in the Railton tradition, started his career with illustrations in Aubrey Beardsley's famous 'decadent' periodical of the 1890s, *The Yellow Book*. He illustrated attractive editions of White's *Selborne* in 1900 and Walton's *Angler* in 1903 and produced an excellent modern version in 1932 of Loggan's bird's-eye *Views of Oxford Colleges*, originally published in the seventeenth century. Will Owen was New's contemporary, but his style was bolder. He is best remembered for his endearing illustrations to W. W. Jacobs's humorous tales of fishing villages, such as *Short Cruises* (1907), which are all bound in brick-red cloth with a pictorial design by Owen stamped in black.

Edward Ardizzone (1900-79), a popular artist, illustrated many children's books but was also successful with volumes such as Le Fanu's *Through a Glass Darkly* (1929), his first book, Dickens's *Great Expectations* (1939), *Ali Baba* (1949) and Stevenson's *Travels with a Donkey* (1967). Equally atmospheric are the illustrations of Mervyn Peake (best known for his Gormenghast trilogy), found in *Hunting of the Snark* (1944) and *Treasure Island* (1949), but his contributions are also widely scattered among the periodicals of the day.

Perhaps the most brilliant of modern line illustrators is Ronald

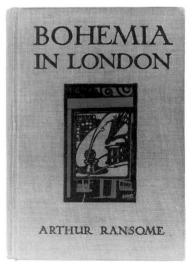

(Left) *A striking Edwardian cloth binding of 1907 designed by Fred Taylor, who also drew the plates inside. Ransome is better known for his children's 'Swallows and Amazons' books.*

Searle, whose wickedly funny schoolgirls first appeared in *Hurrah for St Trinian's* (1948), followed by *Terror of St Trinian's* (1952). For schoolboys he illustrated the Molesworth quartet, *Down with Skool, How to be Topp, Whizz for Atomms* and *Back in the Jug Agane* (1953-9), and for a slightly more sophisticated audience *The Rake's Progress* (1955). He has also contributed to such magazines as *Punch*.

It is essential when collecting these books to obtain copies with the dustjacket, since it will usually bear some extra artwork by the illustrator. Any book in this area of collecting which does not have its dustjacket is incomplete.

Magazines and periodicals

A good way of collecting cheaply a range of British illustrators is to obtain odd examples (complete runs are impossibly bulky) of the many Victorian and Edwardian magazines which flourished in consequence of the Universal Education Act of 1870. Among them may be mentioned *The Graphic, The Temple Magazine, Windsor Magazine, The Idler* and *The Strand Magazine* (in which the Sherlock Holmes stories by Conan Doyle first appear). The formula of such periodicals was to commission special articles and stories from contemporary authors and to illustrate them with drawings by contemporary artists or by photographs. It was a hugely successful formula, and these magazines can still be read with great enjoyment today.

They are found in two formats: firstly (and rarely) in the original monthly parts as issued, with the boldly designed paper wrappers and pages of advertisements; and secondly, in half-yearly or yearly bound volumes in publishers' leather or (preferably) in pictorial cloth. It is also worth watching out for special numbers or bumper Christmas issues, which usually contain a superfluity of good things.

The Studio

One of the most influential periodicals dealing with art, *The Studio*, was founded in 1893 and had an Aubrey Beardsley design on the first wrapper. From the first it devoted space to contemporary book production and this is reflected in *The Studio's* chief glory, the 'Specials' started in 1894 with 'Christmas Cards and Their Designers'. These beautifully produced and instructive volumes, published in wrappers or in cloth as the purchaser preferred, can still be found in bargain basements. Among the most interesting to the book collector are

A wood engraving by V. Le Campion from 'Manon Lescaut' (Folio Society, 1950).

Children's Books (1897), *Modern Bookplates* (1898), *Art of the Book* and *Modern Book Illustrators* (both 1914*), Book Illustration* (1923), *Modern Book Illustration in Britain and America* (1931*), William Morris* (1934), and *The Art of the Book* (1938).

This enterprising house also issued from 1932 an excellent series of *How to Do It* books (about seventy in all), including Claire Leighton and Dorothea Braby on *Wood Engraving* (numbers 2 and 46) in 1932 and 1953, C. F. Tunnicliffe on *Bird Portraiture* (number 35) in 1945, and Rowland Hilder on *Sketching and Painting* (number 67) in 1956.

The Folio Society

This excellent book club, which is still thriving, was founded in 1947 to issue 'great literature in a format worthy of the contents, at a price within the reach of everyman'. The first book, *Tales from Tolstoy*, contained illustrations by Elizabeth MacFadyen, establishing the precedent of using contemporary artists which has been the society's chief contribution to British book production.

Some outstanding works are *Gulliver's Travels*, illustrated by Edward Bawden, and *Shakespeare's Sonnets* decorated by Reynolds Stone, both in 1948, *Poe's Tales*, illustrated by Michael Ayrton in 1957, *Sherlock Holmes* by Paul Hogarth in 1958 and the elegant series of Jane Austen's works in seven volumes issued between 1957 and 1963, illustrated with wood engravings by Joan Hassall, daughter of the artist John Hassall,

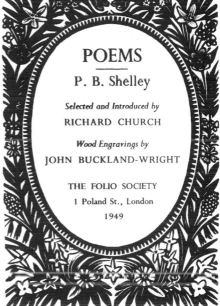

A bold wood-engraved titlepage by J. Buckland-Wright for the Folio Society.

POEMS
——
P. B. Shelley

Selected and Introduced by
RICHARD CHURCH

Wood Engravings by
JOHN BUCKLAND-WRIGHT

THE FOLIO SOCIETY
1 Poland St., London
1949

renowned for his 'Skegness is so bracing' poster. Other illustrators who have worked for the society include Barnet Freedman, Mark Severin, John Lawrence and Charles Keeping, who illustrated Dickens's collected works.

Folio Society books are rarely expensive and the collector can afford to be choosy about condition, waiting for bright, clean copies in the original slipcases (only the earliest titles had dustjackets). A complete list of the society's publications to 1968, together with bibliographical notes on the first editions, is to be found in Folio 21, published by the society in 1968.

Facsimiles

The art of producing exact facsimiles of important books, documents and, above all, of medieval illuminated manuscripts reached a peak of excellence during the 1970s, both in the quality of printing and the materials used, which may not be bettered for a long while. Particularly impressive examples are the three books of hours (prayers to be said at different times of the day) of the Duke of Berry, *Les Très Riches Heures* (1969), *Les Grandes Heures* (1971) and *Les Belles Heures* (1974), all published by Thames & Hudson.

A publication of 1974 by the Scholar Press reproduced with breathtaking realism the pencilled manuscript drafts of Rupert Brooke's poems 'The Fish', 'Grantchester', 'The Dead' and 'The Soldier', now in King's College library. So accurate are the seventeen leaves of facsimiles that even the foxing on the original paper is reproduced! They were published in both a de luxe and a trade issue.

10. Popular editions and series

This is a fruitful field for collectors because these are interesting (and often attractive) examples of innovative publishing methods and materials and are usually inexpensive.

Early collections

In the second half of the eighteenth century, Alexander Donaldson, initially in Edinburgh and later in London, was the first to seriously upset the London publishers with cheap editions of successful works and not to bother himself overmuch about the then comfortable gentlemen's agreements on copyright. But it was John Bell, an enterprising and formidable printer-publisher, typefounder and bookseller, who demonstrated the potential of the cheap reprint, and he did it by expanding, apparently interminably, his reprints by subject series until they must have exhausted public patience. His most famous is *The Poets of Great Britain*, started in 1776 and only concluded, 109 volumes later, in 1792 (and since each volume was much reprinted, odd ones are often to be found). Another of his series is *Bell's British Theatre* in thirty-four volumes, 1776-97. All these are in 12mo format, elegantly printed in small type and with an engraved titlepage and frontispiece.

The nineteenth century

No one publisher was to dominate the cheap reprint market in the nineteenth century as had Bell in the eighteenth and there is a notable increase in original works of literature, science and history specially commissioned for popular series. Archibald Constable brought out his *Constable's Miscellany of Literature, Art & Science* over the years 1826-35, John Murray his *Murray's Family Library* (1829-34) and Colburn & Bentley their *Standard Novels* (1831-54). Later famous publishing names to look out for in this cheap books, serials and periodicals market are John Cassell (*Popular Educator, Illustrated Family Bible*), William & Robert Chambers (*Encyclopaedia, Book of Days*), David Bogue (*European Library*), G. H. Bohn (*Standard, Scientific, and Classical Libraries*), and Charles Knight (*Popular History of England, Penny Cyclopaedia*).

Yellowbacks

Bell's books had been supplied to the trade in sheets or

wrappers to be bound up by the bookseller or his customer, but the *Standard Novels* were trade-bound by the publisher in the newly fashionable cloth, a factor which increasingly made the price less competitive. The eternal search for cost-cutting led some publishers in the 1840s to issue their books casebound in boards, but now, unlike the dull grey boards of the eighteenth century, with pictorial covers gaily printed in colour on (usually) yellow paper-covered boards. They were printed in small type, usually in double columns, sold at a shilling and are, in hindsight, called 'yellowbacks' after their covers. They were sold in vast numbers to working folk of all sorts from tradesmen to parlourmaids, and their biggest market was the second generation of railway travellers so efficiently catered for by W. H. Smith's bookstalls, the first of which was set up at Euston in 1848. One of the most successful yellowback publishers was George Routledge, who actually called his thousand-odd collection *The Railway Library*. Frederick Warne was at one time his partner. The heyday of the yellowback may be said to last from the early 1850s to the late 1870s, after which they started to face competition from wrapper-bound publications, and they all but disappeared around the turn of the century. Colourful and attractive (many later ones were printed by the firm of Edmund Evans), their fragility means that they are rarely found in even good condition, but a display of the top covers makes a spectacular show.

The Cranford series

The Cranford series is the name given, in retrospect, to a number of distinctive reprints of classic tales by Macmillan, who commissioned some fine artists to illustrate them. They are recognisable by the dark green bindings with gilt edges, which have full and rich gilt pictorial blocking on the covers and spine. The first in the series are two Washington Irving titles, *Old Christmas* (1875) and *Bracebridge Hall* (1876), both illustrated by Randolph Caldecott, although the volume which gave its name to the series, *Cranford*, illustrated by Hugh Thomson, was not published until 1891.

Tauchnitz editions

The Tauchnitz *Collection of British and American Authors* was started by Christian Bernhard Tauchnitz of Leipzig in 1841, to supply Continental readers with contemporary English literature. The first in his series was *Pelham* by Bulwer-Lytton

(Left) *The People's edition (1903) of a popular Scottish tale published in wrappers.* (Right) *Another popular tale for sixpence; about the Australian goldfields, it was published in 1913.*

(Lord Lytton) and many famous works by such authors as Dickens, Brontë, Hardy, Eliot and Carlyle followed, the two thousandth title being Morley's *History of English Literature* (1881), which had a special preface by Tauchnitz himself. His English authors were very ready to co-operate with Tauchnitz, even sending advance proofs, because he paid them very well and guaranteed not to sell his editions in Britain or the colonies. By keeping the volumes cheap (they were available in paper or cloth) Tauchnitz sold in huge quantities, made himself a fortune and obtained a barony. His publishing house was destroyed by bombs in the Second World War, although it continued until 1955, having published well over five thousand titles.

Paperbacks

Covering books in paper wrappers is by no means a modern idea, as we have seen on page 70, and Tauchnitz was producing trade paper-bound books throughout the latter half of the nineteenth century. The Edwardian examples in wrappers illustrated above are two of a huge number of popular tales reprinted cheaply with striking covers to attract purchasers and with the endleaves and preliminaries filled with advertisements (usually for cocoa or medical liniments), all to sell at sixpence. Like those shown, they are usually found in poor condition. All of these are better described as 'in wrappers' rather than 'paper-

(Top left) *Irving's 'Rip Van Winkle' (1893) in the Cranford series, with typical dark green cloth, boldly gilt-tooled. The edges are also gilt.* (Top right) *'The Imitation of Christ' by Thomas à Kempis (1937), in the Everyman series, with the decoration by Eric Ravilious.* (Bottom left) *A superb example from the King Penguin series, Fairbank's 'A Book of Scripts' (1949), designed by Jan Tschichold.* (Bottom right) *A title of 1946 in the Britain in Pictures series. This one is by Francis Meynell, the founder of the Nonesuch Press.*

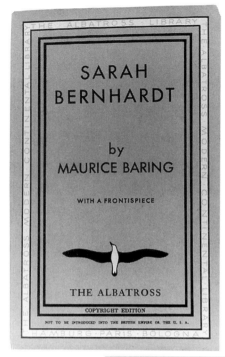

Volume 220 (1934) in the Albatross Modern Continental Library. This one, being biography, is in pink and has its original dustjacket. Below, proof of international co-operation from the colophon.

THIS EDITION IS COMPOSED IN BASKERVILLE TYPE CUT BY THE MONOTYPE CORPORATION. THE PAPER IS SUPPLIED BY MESSRS. LEPARD & SMITHS, LTD., LONDON. THE PRINTING IS EXECUTED BY T. & A. CONSTABLE LTD., OF EDINBURGH, AND THE BINDING IS THE WORK OF OSCAR BRANDSTETTER · ABTEILUNG JAKOB HEGNER · LEIPZIG back', which is a twentieth-century term (the American 'softback' in fact accords better with 'hardback') and may be said to refer to books published from the 1930s onwards and bound in stiffened paper, stronger than wrappers, but still flexible. Curiously, all early paperbacks had dustjackets.

The **Mundanus** imprint formed by Victor Gollancz in 1930 pioneered a series of full-length original novels with what must be considered the first modern paperback, *Gunman* by C. F. Coe. Although designed by the prestigious Stanley Morison, they were not cheap at three shillings, and the series did not flourish, but the experiment was carefully noted in the trade. Soon afterwards, in 1932, the **Albatross Modern Continental Library** was started, with the same idea that Tauchnitz had had a century before, that is to sell paperback reprints of British titles exclusively on the Continent, and for this offices were set up in Hamburg, Paris and Bologna. The first was *The Dubliners* by James Joyce; all the early titles were designed by Giovanni Mardersteig in a Baskerville typeface, printed by Constable in Edinburgh and bound in Leipzig, and they carried a note that they were 'not to be introduced into the British Empire or the U.S.A.'. (In passing we may mention that Mardersteig also ran the celebrated Veronese private press called the Officina Bodoni from 1923 until his death in 1977.) Eventually seven colour-schemes were used for the covers – red for adventure stories, blue for romance etc – and when the venture folded in the 1950s some five thousand titles had been published.

When Allen Lane founded **Penguin Books** in 1935, he took many ideas from Albatross but since, unlike them, he had obtained the rights to sell in Britain and the English-speaking world he profited from immediate bumper sales, made history and his fortune. Ten Penguin titles were published simultaneously in July 1935 at sixpence each, number one in the series being *Ariel* by André Maurois and number ten *Carnival* by Compton Mackenzie. Illogically, *Ariel* has fetched a great deal of money while the other titles issued at the same time, which ought to be equally valuable, are almost overlooked.

In 1937 the same publisher founded **Pelican Books**, designed to publish books of a more philosophical nature, starting with G. B. Shaw's two-volume *Intelligent Woman's Guide to Socialism*. The **Penguin Specials**, also started in 1937, dealt usually with largely political contemporary controversies or interests, but other topics were covered, most notably by Robert

(Left) *The second of ten titles simultaneously issued as the first Penguins in July 1935. This copy has its original dustjacket, orange-coloured like the cover.* (Right) *Volume one of the first volume in the Pelican series (1937). The cover is blue with a white band.*

Gibbings's *Over the Reefs* about coral diving in the South Seas, which was published undated as Penguin Special 16 in 1938, with the hardback following only in 1946.

All Albatross paperbacks right up to the 1950s were properly sewn, but at Penguin in the late 1940s Lane introduced another cost-cutting exercise and had his paperbacks perfect bound, a disaster from a conservation point of view as with the years the gutta-percha often perishes and the books fall apart.

King Penguins

Another example of the enterprise of Allen Lane, the King Penguins were started in 1939 to provide attractive but inexpensive illustrated pocket-size hardback books on a variety of topics, with an authoritative text by an expert. The first was P. Barclay Smith's *British Birds*, which was illustrated with coloured plates after those of John Gould, a celebrated Victorian ornithologist. The series concentrated on natural history, but heraldry, art, ballet, calligraphy and archaeology were all covered in the seventy-six volumes which make up a complete set. Some particularly noteworthy titles are Edward Bawden's *Life in an English Village* (1949), John Piper's *Romney Marsh*

(1950) and Ronald Searle's *John Gilpin* (1953). The last in the series was *Sculptures of the Parthenon* by P. Corbett, published in 1959. The twenty-eight titles published from 1949 onwards have dustjackets.

Britain in Pictures

This series was similar in concept to the King Penguins, but more topical and in larger format. All one hundred and twenty-six titles were first published between 1941 and 1947 by Collins, but most were subsequently reprinted. Many of the topics in the list are highly original and informative: *British Rebels and Reformers* (1942); *British Trade Unions* (1942); *Women's Institutes* (1943); *British Red Cross* (1944); and *Horses of Britain* (1944). Sport and literature are well covered: *English Cricket* (1945); *British Golf* (1946); *English Letter Writers* (1945); and *English Essayists* (1946).

The series also contains some titles by important writers – Edmund Blunden on *English Villages* (1941); Kate O'Brien on *English Diarists* (1943); John Betjeman on *English Cities* (1943); and George Orwell on *The English People* (1947). Several poets were covered in the series, for example Tennyson, Wordsworth and Shelley, but these were issued in a slightly smaller format than usual. Occasionally related subjects were gathered into a collected volume, such as *British Adventure*, *Literature* and *Craftsmanship*, but these are curiously neglected by collectors.

Everyman series

The famous Everyman series of reprints of classics was begun in 1906 by J. M. Dent with *Boswell's Johnson* in two volumes. They were issued in cloth at one shilling or leather at two shillings, and each had a richly decorative titlepage in the Kelmscott Press tradition designed by R. L. Knowles, but this was replaced in the 1930s with designs by Eric Ravilious. From the start they were hugely popular, the first hundred and fifty titles selling two million copies in the first year, and the list contained some well-known contemporary authors – G. K. Chesterton, A. C. Swinburne and Hilaire Belloc – as well as talented illustrators such as Arthur Rackham (with *Gulliver* and *Lamb's Tales*), R. Anning Bell (Grimms' *Fairy Tales*) and T. H. Robinson (*Tom Brown* and *Book of Saints*).

Dent was no newcomer to publishing for the popular market. In 1894-6 he had issued the enormously successful *Temple*

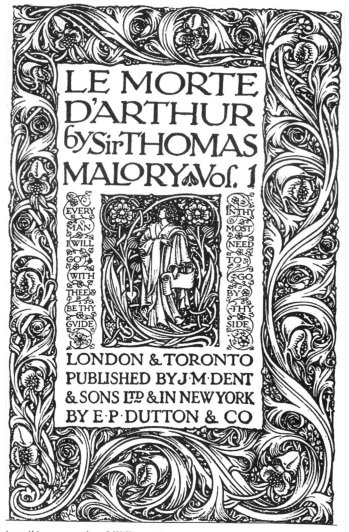

A striking example of William Morris's influence on commercial book production is the titlepage that was used for the first volumes in the Everyman series; the one illustrated is from 1906 and was designed by R. L. Knowles.

Shakespeare, a pocket edition of forty volumes at one shilling each edited by Sir Israel Gollancz. Each volume was printed in black and red on handmade paper with a titlepage designed by Walter Crane, and the reissue (1934-6) was designed by Eric Gill, who also designed the endpapers for *Collins Illustrated Pocket Classics* of 1936.

The Saturday Books

Usually quite saucy and always colourful and interesting, the Saturday Books abound with original contributions and illustrations by the foremost writers and illustrators of the day – Bates, Steinbeck, Sassoon, Graves, Greene, Sitwell, Gibbings, Searle, A. Miller Parker and others – and are good fun to collect. There are thirty-four volumes in a complete set, edited variously by Leonard Russell and John Hadfield, one volume being published every year between 1941 and 1974. All but the earliest volumes bear a colourful dustjacket and latterly each volume was supplied with a handsome box.

'Discovering' books

We cannot leave this section without a mention of the Shire 'Discovering' series, which started with *Discovering East Suffolk* in 1962, a slim volume of 24 pages, printed in an edition of 10,000 copies to be distributed free at petrol stations, tourist information centres and the like and which was collated and stapled by hand. Six other topographical guides followed in six years, but *Discovering Brasses and Brass Rubbing* in 1967 set the pattern of concise guides to all sorts of interesting and unusual subjects, written by experts. Of the two hundred and eighty-nine titles published to date a good number are, or were in their day, the only book on their subject readily available: *English Fairs, Bells and Bellringing, Horse Brasses* (all 1968), *Topiary, Traction Engines, Lifeboats* (all 1969), *Corn Dollies* (1974), *Farmhouse Cheese* (1978), to mention just a few. *Playing Cards and Tarots* of 1972 was the first to be numbered (142) and previous titles were then numbered retrospectively.

11. Modern first editions

Many people find the very thought of first editions frightening, speaking of them in reverential tones and assuming that they are all rare and expensive, obtainable only by the very wealthy and knowledgeable, and are never to be handled. But this is far from true: first editions are usually very easy to distinguish, and many have no value whatever. Only when the text itself has proved to be of consequence or if the text is by an author of consequence does the first edition of that text assume some interest and, it may be, value. Even then, some books in these categories may be so common in first edition or their authors so out of fashion that their commercial value is small, and an example is the posthumously published *More Poems* of 1936 by A. E. Housman of *Shropshire Lad* fame. *A Shropshire Lad*, by contrast, is a very valuable book, having been published in an edition of only 350 copies, in 1896.

How to tell a first edition

A first edition is any volume of original matter not previously published. It can usually be recognised because the publisher will put the date of publication alone at the foot of the title page or he will put the date with other information on the verso of the title page, sometimes in the form of a short note like the following, which occurs in the first edition of *The Go-Between* by L. P. Hartley: 'First published in Great Britain, 1953'. If this is all the information given it is usually safe to assume that the book is a first edition.

If a reprint or new impression is called for, it will usually be acknowledged as such. Thus a reprint of T. S. Eliot's play *The Cocktail Party* has the following on the verso of the title:

> First published March MCML
> Second Impression April MCML
> Third Impression May MCML.

The first reprint of E. M. Forster's *A Passage to India* has the titlepage with the date 1924 at the foot exactly as in the first edition but has the words 'Second impression' overprinted in the centre, and this is the only apparent difference between the two impressions.

A collector is usually only interested in the *first impression* of

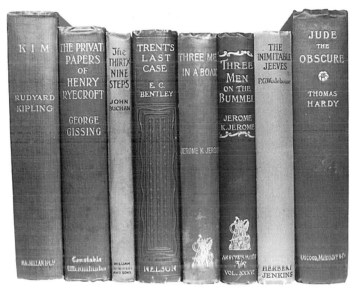

First editions of volumes rarely found with dustjackets: (left to right) 1901, 1903, 1915, [1912], 1889, 1900, 1923, 1896.

the first edition, and this is understood in the term 'first edition' whenever it is used by dealers. However, some collectors are interested in second or subsequent impressions because they may contain minor amendments to the text and may sometimes, like Forster's *A Room with a View*, be even scarcer than the first impression.

New editions are also of interest to the collector of books by a particular author for they may embody substantial alterations and additions or alter the original format.

Undated books

One should always be suspicious of an undated book: it is likely to be a reprint. But unfortunately some first editions were published undated, the publishers Nelson and Hodder & Stoughton being notorious in this respect. Nelson published that classic tale of detective fiction *Trent's Last Case* by E. C. Bentley [1913] in post octavo format, in royal blue cloth and with a coloured frontispiece but without a date; and Hodder & Stoughton were particularly hard on Edgar Wallace collectors, issuing eleven first editions by him in 1926, all of them un-dated! In these cases careful detective work is needed: studying bibliographies, publishers' lists and other copies; and even the printed list of publishers' other titles often found opposite the titlepage or at the end of the book may be of help in fixing the date.

States or variants

If changes are made to the text of a book during the course of printing and before any part of the edition has been published (i.e. put on sale to the public) then it will be available in two states, one before the changes and one after them. An example is T. S. Eliot's *The Wasteland*, published in New York in 1922: the first state has the word 'mountain' correctly in place on page 43, whereas in the second state it has dropped out of place. Both states were published (though not printed) at the same time so there is no priority between them and there is no point in preferring one to the other.

Issues

If part of an edition is already published when some changes are made to the remaining copies, internally or externally, then two issues become discernible. The first issue is all those copies sold before the changes were made; the second issue is all copies which incorporate the change.

In Robert Graves's *Goodbye to All That* (1929), the first issue contains on page 341 a poem by Sassoon printed without that poet's permission. This was replaced by asterisks in the second issue when Sassoon had complained only after some copies had been published.

Issue points may also occur in the bindings of books, and the one important work of that curious character Frederick Rolfe, who called himself 'Baron Corvo', namely *Hadrian the Seventh* (1904), is a good example. The upper cover of the first edition bears a design by Rolfe himself of Pope Hadrian with his arm raised in benediction: in the first issue this design is stamped in white, but in the second it is blind-stamped. Another example is *Biography for Beginners* [1905] by E. Clerihew [Bentley], the work which introduced the word *clerihew* into the language. It was illustrated by G. K. Chesterton and the first issue is in quarter grey cloth with his pictorial boards, while the second issue is in green paper covers with the (misleading) words 'Popular edition 2s 6d net' on the upper cover.

De luxe issues

Some authors have a habit of issuing some of their books in signed de luxe copies, and very often these will be difficult and expensive to buy. But since they are usually issued simultaneously with the ordinary or trade copies the de luxe issues are not essential items for the collector of first editions, although they certainly are desirable, being printed in attractive format, limited in number and usually signed by the author.

A notable enthusiast for the private issue was the First World War poet Siegfried Sassoon, whose *The Heart's Journey*, designed by Bruce Rogers in 1927, and *Rhymed Ruminations*, Chiswick Press, 1939, did precede the ordinary editions of 1929 and 1940.

International priorities

It often happens that where a title is to be published in two countries (say the United States and Britain) the publication date for the two editions is not the same, and it is an inflexible rule that wherever a book first appears then that edition of the book is the true first. So, although Richard Hughes's bestselling *High Wind in Jamaica* was published in London in 1929, this is the first British edition, since it was preceded (by months only) by the true first edition published in New York as *The Innocent Voyage*.

Many collectors, however, preferring sentiment to logic, collect the first edition to appear in the author's own country, true first or not, and this understandable weakness is described as 'following the flag'.

Proof and association copies

When a new book is set up ready for printing, fifteen to twenty copies will usually be run off to give to the author, publisher and even newspaper editors for last minute checking, correction or advance reviews. These prefigurations of the finished book are very desirable to author-collectors, although they are usually well thumbed and the paper wrappers damaged. Sometimes the author's own corrected proof occurs for sale with his manuscript amendments and these are not to be missed.

Association copies are volumes in which a great part of the interest lies in a link between the author of the book, a character or place in the book and a previous owner of the book. An example would be Paul Schofield's copy of *A Man for All Seasons* (1961), by Robert Bolt, because Schofield played Sir

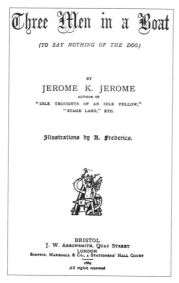

The first issue of the first edition. In later issues the number 11 is added to the address in the fifth line from the bottom.

Thomas More in the film of the book; another would be an inscribed copy from the author of Jerome's *Three Men in a Boat* (1889), to Carl Hentschel, since he was the original for Harris in that book.

Condition

It is very important with modern first editions that they be in good clean condition and with the dustjacket, if possible (see chapter 7). Copies with ugly inscriptions (except by the author) or with former library labels and marks should be avoided at all costs.

Book club editions

The importance of book clubs in disseminating literature of all sorts in the twentieth century is beyond question. The idea is to commit a member to purchasing a set number of books selected every year by the club and offered to him well below the published price. Publishers welcomed the idea because it guaranteed them a certain volume of sales, but in order to protect the regular book market the clubs had to issue their books using cheaper paper and bindings and with fewer illustrations, if there were any, put the club imprint on the titlepage and spine and make it quite clear that their editions were not

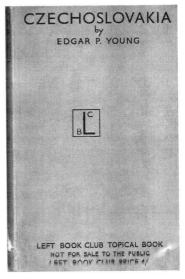

A typical title from the Left Book Club. This one, being 'topical' (the date is 1938), is in red boards, not the usual orange wrappers.

CZECHOSLOVAKIA
by
EDGAR P. YOUNG

LEFT BOOK CLUB TOPICAL BOOK
NOT FOR SALE TO THE PUBLIC
LEFT BOOK CLUB PRICE 1/

available in bookshops. Nowadays, however, publishers often run off the club copies themselves and the only difference between club books and the publisher's own might be a sticker covering the imprint on the titlepage. Rather illogically, since they are sometimes published simultaneously with the publisher's version, book club editions are still not usually noticed in bibliographies and it would be interesting and inexpensive to collect first book-club editions of important works by famous authors.

The first club, the Book of the Month Club, was founded in the USA in 1926, with the Literary Guild following in 1927. Other well-known clubs include the Book Society, the Companion Book Club and the Readers' Union. The Left Book Club, founded in the 1930s, with the books bound in very distinctive orange wrappers, was rather different in that they commissioned new works and reprinted others, all with a socialist viewpoint. The first edition of George Orwell's *The Road to Wigan Pier* was issued by them in 1937. See also the Folio Society (chapter 9).

What to collect

A popular method of book collecting is to choose an author and try to assemble a complete collection of his published

The titlepage to the first edition of George Bernard Shaw's 'The Adventures of the Black Girl' (1932). The whole design is by John Farleigh.

works (a particularly ambitious collector will also try to buy unpublished letters and manuscripts). This means not only buying the first editions and important subsequent editions of his books, but also scouring likely periodicals for the author's contributions, and it is in this field that the collector can often find himself in a pioneering role.

Usually an author's first book will be the most difficult to find, because the print run of an unknown author is likely to have been small, and it may be expensive, but the collector must take a deep breath and buy when the opportunity arises, for it may not recur for a long time and then the price will probably have increased. For example, the collector of William Golding's works will have little difficulty with most of his books, such as *Free Fall* (1959), *The Spire* (1964) and *The*

Pyramid (1967), but Golding's *Poems* of 1934 and *Lord of the Flies* (1954) will both take considerable effort to find.

Other collectors like to pick a period, say the poetry of the 1930s with Auden, MacNeice, Spender and Dylan Thomas, or the works of the 'angry young men' of the 1950s, John Braine, Colin Wilson and John Osborne. Some collectors might be interested in the spy story from James Bond in *Casino Royale* (1953) to Len Deighton's *Ipcress File* (1962) and John Le Carré's *Spy Who Came In from the Cold* (1963); or in English drama from Dylan Thomas's *Under Milk Wood* (1954) to Peter Shaffer's *Equus* (1973); or in books which have been filmed, such as John Wyndham's *Day of the Triffids* (1951) or Anthony Burgess's *Clockwork Orange* (1962). Still others will browse among the productions of the past fifty years and pick out first editions of books which seem important or influential – Evelyn Waugh's trilogy *Men at Arms* (1952), *Officers and Gentlemen* (1954) and *Unconditional Surrender* (1961), or Kingsley Amis's *Lucky Jim* (1953). And one should not forget the collector of first editions *in* English (not the same thing as 'first English edition') of foreign authors; for example Federico Garcia Lorca's *Poems* translated by Stephen Spender and J. L. Gill, London (1939) or *Three Tragedies; Blood Wedding, Yerma, Bernada Alba,* translated by R. O'Connell and J. Graham-Lujan, New York (1947).

Where to begin

Before embarking on collecting a particular author it is useful to draw up a checklist of his published works, which can be ticked off as they are acquired. Most local libraries will have a reference section and if it does not contain a bibliography of your particular author it will have such standard works as *The Dictionary of National Biography*, *Who Was Who*, *The Cambridge Bibliography of English Literature* and possibly the *Catalogue of the British Library* collections, one of which will certainly list his publications.

Further information may be obtained from an author's publisher or a library which has specialised in collecting that author (such as Walsall Public Library, which has a fine collection of Jerome K. Jerome), or from such admiring societies which may have been founded to further study into one author (the addresses can usually be found in telephone directories).

12. Ideas

In a book this size it has been possible to mention only a few of the hundreds of subjects that people collect, from railway books and timetables to geology, wireless (before 1930), television (before 1950), cookery and music, but let us look briefly at two popular subjects and offer a few ideas to finish.

Sports

There are two famous series dedicated to the subject. The first is *The Badminton Library of Sports & Pastimes*, edited by the Duke of Beaufort and A. E. T. Watson and published by Longmans between 1886 and the 1920s, with reprints and new editions. They are handsome books, the ordinary issues bound in brown pictorial cloth and full of wood engravings in the text and full-page, and it would be hard to think of a subject not

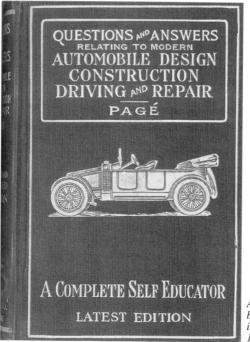

An attractive binding on an interesting book of 1921.

covered in the seventy or so volumes – cycling, dancing, hunting, driving etc. The other series, edited by the Earl of Lonsdale, is *The Lonsdale Library of Sports, Games and Pastimes*, the first of which was *Horsemanship* by G. Brooke (1929). Volume 27, *Motor Racing* by Earl Howe, had been reached by 1939, when the Second World War broke out, and the series was not resumed afterwards. Both collections offered purchasers two or three alternative bindings. The *Fur, Fin and Feather* series, published 1893-1906 and also edited by A. E. T. Watson, was dedicated to hunting and fishing and eventually comprised twelve volumes. Various authors contributed articles to make up each volume and the last article tells how to cook what you have caught. Two other important publishers of sporting books were Methuen and A. & C. Black and the advertisement leaflets illustrated give an idea of the books available in the 1920s.

Ever the first port of call for the beginner is the subject entry in a good encyclopedia. If he looks up skiing, for example, he will probably find the name of Arnold Lunn, an important early promoter of the sport. By checking the British Library Catalogue he will see that Lunn wrote at least eight books on the subject, from *Ski-ing* (1913) to *The Story of Ski-ing* (1953). If he checks for cricket he will see that Wisden's *Cricketer's Almanac* was started as long ago as 1864; for fishing, that in 1653 was published not only the first book on the subject but also a classic of English literature, *The Compleat Angler* by Izaac Walton. Luckily, as it is rare, there are a number of facsimiles of the first edition – that by Elliot Stock (1896), being one of the best – as well as hundreds of other editions, many of them illustrated, including one by Arthur Rackham (1931).

Natural history

Antique natural history books are among the most attractive ever produced, owing to the copper, wood and steel engravings or lithographs that often illustrate them, and especially when these are coloured by hand. Among the most impressive are the forty-one imperial folio volumes published between 1832 and 1881 by John Gould, 'the bird man'. These are expensive books, but no one could complain that they are not getting their money's worth: each volume measures $15\frac{1}{2}$ by $22\frac{1}{2}$ inches (40 by 55 cm) and contains up to ninety beautiful hand-coloured lithograph plates of birds, some of them by Gould's wife, Elizabeth, and some by Edward Lear of 'nonsense' fame. Wilfrid Blunt's standard study of botanical pictures and plates,

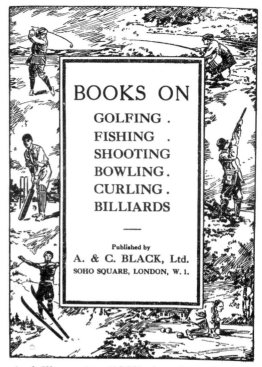

(Right and opposite page) *Two publishers' advertisements for sporting books, 1920s.*

BOOKS ON

GOLFING .
FISHING .
SHOOTING
BOWLING .
CURLING .
BILLIARDS

—

Published by
A. & C. BLACK, Ltd.
SOHO SQUARE, LONDON, W. 1.

The Art of Botanical Illustration (1950), is volume 14 of a famous and much collected series, the *Collins New Naturalist Monographs*, the first of which, *Butterflies* by E. B. Ford, came out in 1945. Some of the subjects are very original, D. Morley's *Ants* (1953), G. Butler's *Honeybee* (1954), and K. Mellanby's *The Mole* (1971), to choose three at random. These are the dates of the first editions, but all were reprinted over the years.

Other themes

One of the most rewarding aspects of book collecting is developing a theme for your collection that has not been systematically attacked before. Some careful thought and a little research are needed so that a rough plan can be formed for assembling such a collection, although this will inevitably be altered and adapted as the interest develops.

Books which are important because they discuss or demonstrate in themselves some advance in technology are continually being produced and may be collected by the alert while still cheap. Two examples are the first book in Britain to be filmset (printed from transparent sheets bearing a photographic image of the text), which was Linklater's *Private Angelo*, printed in an edition of two thousand copies in 1957, and the first book to be computer typeset (that is with the type for the whole text arranged by computer), which was Margaret Drabble's *Millstone* (1965). On a less serious level, the first book to have different smells is *The Romantic Story of Scent* by John Trueman (1975), which has several pads on the dustjacket which smell of lavender, orange and so on when scratched lightly!

Books bearing as illustrations actual tipped-in photographs are now hotly collected, but it might still be possible to obtain the *Art Union* of 1846 at a low price; it contains the first photograph in any magazine. Curiously, volumes of poetry with original photographs are often neglected, and some volumes of poetry by Scott, Wordsworth and Tennyson dating from the 1870s contain most interesting photographic views of subjects mentioned in the poems.

13. Glossary of terms

Art paper: the shiny, polished paper at first used for plates only, but now any art book is usually printed throughout on this paper, which has a thin coating of china clay. The earliest use the present author has noticed are some plates in *The Recreation, A Gift Book for Young Readers* (1841).

Association copy: a copy of a book in which the main interest is some definable link between the book itself and any previous owner. It may be the author's own copy with his notes, the dedicatee's copy, the copy of Mr X who is mentioned on page 27, or any number of variables.

Binder's cloth: an inferior cloth or buckram binding probably commissioned by a library and not by the original publisher, and so not having the publisher's imprint on the spine.

Black-letter: the 'gothic' typeface, preferred by printers until the end of the sixteenth century, since when roman is standard. Black-letter bibles always seem to have more flavour than those in roman.

Blank: a leaf which is part of a gathering but bears no printing.

Blind-stamped: where the binder's tool is pressed into the leather or cloth without the gold leaf, so leaving an impression in blind.

Blurb: a term invented in the 1920s for comments about the book, from the press, authors or publishers, printed on the fold-in of a dustjacket. Stanley Morison daringly carried them on to the front of the jacket in the 1930s.

Boards or original boards: the cardboard covers used as a cheap publisher's binding before cloth.

Broadside: a sheet printed on one side only; usually a proclamation or ballad.

Buckram: a hard-wearing waxed cloth, much used in public libraries for rebinding.

Calf: a smooth luxurious skin, the most commonly used leather after morocco.

Cancel: a leaf or leaves separately printed to replace a badly or incorrectly printed leaf in the book. The leaf to be replaced (the *cancelland*) is torn out and discarded and the cancel is tipped in in its place.

Casebound: the trade binding of most modern books in cloth or boards, where the sewn or glued gatherings are encased in the covers with hinges of paper or muslin rather than sewn in on cords as with older books or craft bookbindings.

Catchword: in older books, a word printed at the foot of one page which is repeated as the first word on the following page and thereby aids collation.

Chromolithography: printing in colours by lithography (with stone blocks), common in Victorian and Edwardian books as an alternative to wood engravings printed in colours, and superseded by half-tone.

Collate, collation: a careful checking, of signatures, pages, plates etc, of the contents of a book, usually comparing the copy in hand with a bibliography.

Colophon: gives the details of printing at the foot of the last page, now superseded by the titlepage, but retained for some press books.

Conjugate: leaves that are joined at the inner fold are said to be conjugate.

Contemporary: used of bindings or inscriptions made within about fifteen years of the book's publication.

Copperplate: etched or engraved illustrations in books, printed from coppers, in greatest numbers in the seventeenth and eighteenth centuries.

Damp-stained: a term of abuse. Exposure to damp leaves yellow-brown patches on the paper and helps to rot it.

Disbound: usually of pamphlets removed from a bound collection.

Dog-eared: the deplorable habit of folding down, at various intervals, a corner of the leaf to mark one's place leaves a book 'dog-eared'.

Double-column: where the text is printed in two columns side by side on each page: common in Bibles.

Dustjacket or dustwrapper: the printed paper covering wrapped round the book.

Edges: the edges of a volume may be *coloured* (usually red, but sometimes yellow or green); *sprinkled* with red ink spots; *gilt* with gold leaf; *marbled; trimmed;* or *uncut* (left untouched by the binder).

Edition: any number of copies of a book printed off in any number of printing operations from the same setting of type without substantial change. New impressions and reprints are still part of the same edition since they are printed off from unaltered type. Only substantial changes or resetting of type can constitute a new edition (see also *First edition* and *Impression*).

Edition de luxe: a volume printed for the connoisseur in small numbers and using carefully chosen materials.

Endpapers: the paper sides which are stuck on the inside of the covers (*pastedowns*) and the conjugate leaf (*free endpaper*) which forms the first and last blank leaf in the book.

Engraving, engraved plates: the plates or vignettes in a book which have been printed from intaglio or incised designs on copper, steel or wood.

Extra: as in 'gilt extra'; of leather bindings, denoting more decorative gilt tooling than usual.

Extra-illustrated: when additional relevant engraved portraits, views etc have been bound up to illustrate a volume of history or topography. Also called *grangerised* after the Reverend James Granger (1723-76), whose book and recommendations started the fashion.

First edition: the first printing of any work from the manuscript or typescript. To book collectors this means the first *impression* of the first edition.

Fly-leaf: also called the front free endpaper. The first blank leaf attached to the paste-down endpaper.

Fly-title: the short printed title immediately before the text in some older books.

Foxed, foxing: the small rust-coloured freckles sometimes found on the pages or edges of books.

Frontispiece: the first plate in a book, opposite the titlepage.

Gathering: when one sheet has been printed on both sides, folded and sewn into the book, the leaves from that sheet belong to one gathering, which is sewn through the centre fold. Each gathering in the book is given its own signature letter.

Gilt edges: where the edges of (usually) leather-bound books have been coated with gold.

Glosses: marginal notes.

Half-bound: a volume with the spine and corners in leather, the space between covered in cloth or marbled paper.

Half-title: the leaf before the titlepage which bears a shortened version of that title and sometimes (on the verso) the printer's name.

Half-tone: a photographic printing process in black and white or colour dating from the 1880s which uses plates made up of different-sized dots to produce tones.

Headband: a thin strip of coloured silk threads found on the inside of the head and tail of the spine, usually, but not always, on craft bookbindings (see illustration page 64).

Hinge: the hinge inside the covers.

Impression: any copies from a batch of books printed off in one continuous operation. An *edition* can comprise any number of separate impressions but the collector is usually interested in only the first.

Imprint: the publisher's name (and sometimes address) at the foot of the titlepage; the 'printer's imprint' is usually on the verso.

India paper: a thin, almost tissue, paper much used for Bibles and prayer books. Actually it used to come from China.

Issue: sometimes it happens that changes are made to a book after part of the edition has already been published (i.e. offered for sale to the public) and in this case two or more issues are discernible. The first issues will be copies sold before the change was made; the second or later issues will be of copies which incorporate the change. Collectors will usually be more interested in a first issue than any later issues.

Italic: *this cursive type; first used by the Venetian printer Aldus in 1501.*

Japanese paper: a thick, vellum-like paper much used for Edwardian illustrated books in de luxe editions.

Joints: the outside hinges of a book cover; they may be 'tender' or 'cracked'.

Large paper copy: one of a small number of superior copies printed off on fine paper of greater than usual dimensions, so giving the bound book wide margins.

Leaf: has two pages, one each on the *recto* and *verso*. It may be 'missing and supplied in facsimile'.

Lithograph: plates printed from designs drawn by the artist on the surface of smooth blocks of limestone. Invented by Aloys Senefelder in 1798.

Marbled calf: a pattern etched in calf bindings with acids, sometimes giving a 'tree' shape on each board, hence *tree-calf.*

Marbled paper: patterned paper (above) used for endpapers and covers.

Miniature book: any book under about 3 inches (76 mm) in height.

Morocco: a grainy, hard-wearing but sumptuous leather used for most craft bookbinding. It is the skin of a goat and is still imported from Morocco.

Mounted at large: of colour plates or photographs when they are tipped on to a larger leaf, usually of paper of a different colour and thickness. Common in the books of Rackham, Dulac *et al.*

Offsets, offsetting: unpleasant brown staining found on the page opposite an engraved plate and mirroring the engraving.

Page: one printed side of a leaf.

Pamphlet: a publication with a small number of leaves only.

Panelled: of bindings, usually seventeenth- or eighteenth-century calf, where a central double rectangle is ruled with blind lines on each cover.

Perfect bound: a binding for paperbacks where the backs of the sections are cut flush, glued rather than sewn, and set in the covers.

Plates: for book collectors this means the full-page illustrations printed on separate paper from that of the text and pasted in. But it also can mean the metal sheets bearing the engraved design from which the plates in the book were printed.

Preliminaries: the half-title, titlepage, contents leaves and fly-title, i.e. the first leaves in the book.

Proof: a proof copy is a sample volume printed off (and usually bound in wrappers) before the main print run, for the author, publishers and others to check.

Proof plates: will often be lettered as such. They are the earliest pulls from the engraved copper or steel and will have the best impression; often the title of the print has still to be added.

Provenance: a note on previous owners.

Published edition: as in *First [published] Edition*, means that this first edition available to the general public was preceded by a privately issued or suppressed edition.

Quarter-bound: a volume with just the spine in leather; the sides are covered in cloth or marbled paper.

Rebacked: where a binder has replaced the original spine with a new one; he may sometimes have incorporated part of the original.

Recased: where a binder has resewn a volume which has worked loose and reset it into the original covers. The endpapers will sometimes have been replaced.

Recto: the front side of any leaf, i.e. the right-hand page in an opened book (opposite of *verso*).

Rubricated: with the initials filled out by hand in red. Some devotional works are also *ruled in red*, i.e. have hand-drawn red lines dividing the printed columns and headings.

Signature: the letter assigned to a gathering or section, found at the foot of the first page of the first leaf of any gathering.

Slipcase: a protective cardboard casing into which a book slips snugly, leaving the spine on view. A ribbon pull or finger cut-outs on the side sometimes aid removal of the volume.

Speckled or sprinkled: where the calf binding has been sprinkled with acid to give a dappled effect. Also used on the edges of books.

Square brackets: [ ] used when the information contained within does not appear on the book itself but is deduced or known from other sources.

Subscriber's copy: an early copy purchased by an original subscriber to a published work.

Thumbed: an obvious term for a very well read book which will have stains of finger grease and battered leaves.

Ties: the ribbons sometimes attached to the upper and lower covers of a book to hold them together over the fore-edge. Usually mentioned only if one is missing.

Titlepage or titleleaf: the page or leaf at the beginning of a book which bears details of the author, publisher and date of publication.

Trade: 'the trade' is bookselling and booksellers or publishers; 'rarely seen in the trade', 'trade binding'.

Tree-calf: see *Marbled calf.*

Unbound: a book or pamphlet which has never been bound; it may still be stitched as issued.

Uncut or deckle: where the edges of the pages are not trimmed by the binder but left rough.

Unopened: where the folds at the tops and some edges of the leaves have not been cut open.

Unsophisticated: an antique that is in wholly original condition throughout.

Verso: the back page of any one leaf, i.e. the left-hand page of any opened book (the opposite of *recto*).

Vignette: a small engraved scene without a border, often placed in the centre of the titlepage.

Washed: usually of plates soaked in bleach to clean out any staining; they should then have been thoroughly rinsed to ensure that the paper will not rot.

Watered or moiré silk: a patterned silk sometimes used for luxurious covers, endpapers or slipcases.

Watermark: the maker's mark in a sheet of paper, seen by holding the leaf up to the light.

Wrappers: flimsy paper covers for pamphlets or slighter books.

Roman numerals

A cumbersome system of dating found on most books before 1800. Each numeral has to be added mentally to arrive at the total, thus: X = 10, XX = 20, XXX = 30, XXXI = 31, XXXVI = 36.

M = 1000	I = 1	VI = 6
D = 500	II = 2	VII = 7
C = 100	III = 3	VIII = 8
L = 50	IV = 4	IX = 9
	V = 5	X = 10

Some examples: MCCCCLXXV = 1475; MDXXXIII = 1533;
MDCXLVI = 1646 (the X before the L has to be subtracted);
MDCCLXXXVIII = 1788; MDCCCXII = 1812; MDCCCCLXXXI
or MCMLXXXI = 1981.

Bibliography

Many books mentioned include a reference bibliography for further study. All imprints are London unless otherwise stated.

Chapter 1: Introduction to printing and terminology
Authors such as W. W. R. Greg, Fredson Bowers and R. B. McKerrow are the pioneering authorities on the hand-printing era but their studies, although still of interest, have been assimilated, revised and updated to include machine printing in what is now the standard work:

Gaskell, P. *A New Introduction to Bibliography*. Clarendon Press, Oxford, 1972, reprinted with corrections 1985.

A straightforward but informative short introduction to the complexities of modern (but pre-computer) book production:

Carey, D. *Printing Processes*. Ladybird Books, Loughborough, 1971.

Chapter 2: Practical experience

Baynes-Cope, A. D. *Caring for Books and Documentation* British Library, second edition 1989.

The British Library formula dressing for leather-bound books is available from Henry Sotheran Ltd, 2-5 Sackville Street, London WC1X 2DP (telephone: 0171-439 6151).

Chapter 3: The history of early printing

Ing, J. *Johann Gutenberg and His Bible*. British Library, 1990.
Pollard, A. *Fine Books*. 1912; reprint, EP Publishing, Wakefield, 1973.

Two books on printing in the whole of Europe:

Clair, C. *A History of European Printing*. Academic Press, reprint 1981.
Steinberg, S. H. *Five Hundred Years of Printing*. 1955; revised edition, British Library, 1996.

Chapter 4: From Caxton to Dickens

Duff, E. Gordon. *Fifteenth Century English Books*. Oxford University Press, reprinted 1964.
Painter, G. D. *William Caxton*. Chatto & Windus, 1976.

Two indispensable reference works which fully list (with dates, editions and location of copies) all recorded books printed in Britain and books in English printed abroad to 1800 are:

Pollard, A. F., and Redgrave, G. R. *A Short-Title Catalogue of Books Printed in England, Scotland and Ireland, 1475-1640*. Second edition in three volumes revised and enlarged, Oxford University Press, 1976-91. (Known as 'STC'.)

BIBLIOGRAPHY

Wing, D. G. *A Short-Title Catalogue of Books Printed in England etc., 1641-1700.* Second edition in three volumes, revised and enlarged, Modern Language Association of America, 1973-5. (Known as 'Wing'.)

A continuation of the Short-Title Catalogue for the eighteenth century is available online from the British Library.

Two important bibliographical catalogues:

Rothschild Library (The). *A Catalogue of 18th Century Printed Books and Manuscripts Formed by Lord Rothschild.* 1954; reprint, Dawson, Folkestone, 1993.
Sadleir, M. *XIX Century Fiction, a Bibiliographical Record.* Constable, two volumes, 1951.

Bibles: the standard catalogue and a general account.

Herbert, A. S. *Historical Catalogue of Printed Editions of the English Bible 1525-1961* (expanded from 'Darlow and Moule'). British and Foreign Bible Society, 1968.
Wheeler Robinson, H. (editor). *The Bible in Its Ancient and English Versions.* Clarendon Press, Oxford, 1940.

Other works:

Bennett, H. S. *English Books and Readers, 1475-1640.* Cambridge University Press, three volumes, 1950-70, with reprints and revised editions.
Jaggard, W. *Shakespeare Bibliography.* A dictionary of every known issue of the writings. Shakespeare Press, Stafford, 1911.
Mumby, F. *Publishing and Bookselling.* Jonathan Cape, 1930.
The New Cambridge Bibliography of English Literature. Cambridge University Press, revised edition in five volumes, 1974-7.
The Oxford Companion to English Literature (editor M. Drabble). Oxford University Press, fifth edition 1985.
Plant, M. *The English Book Trade.* Allen & Unwin, third edition 1974.
Pollard, G. *Serial Fiction: Aspects of Book Collecting.* Constable, 1934.

There are monographic bibliographies of, amongst many others, the Baskerville and Foulis presses, of Johnson, Scott, Austen, Trollope and Dickens (parts and cloth).

Chapter 5: Travel and topographical books

Abbey, J. R. *Travel in Aquatint and Lithography, 1770-1860, from the Library of J. R. Abbey* (two volumes). 1956; reprinted, Alan Wofsy Fine Arts, San Francisco, 1991.
Casada, J. *An Annotated Bibliography of Exploration in Africa.* Oxford University Press, 1992.
Tooley, R. V. *English Books with Coloured Plates, 1790-1860.* Batsford, 1954; reprinted 1987.
Upcott, W. *Bibliographical Account of...English Topography* (three volumes). 1818; reprinted, EP Publishing, Wakefield, 1978.

See also Hunnisett (chapter 9).

Chapter 6: Children's books

Darton, F. J. H. *Children's Books in England. Five Centuries of Social Life.* Cambridge University Press, 1932; reprinted 1960.

Eyre, F. *20th-Century Children's Books 1900-1950.* Longmans, 1952.

Muir, Percy. *English Children's Books 1600-1900.* Batsford, 1954; reprinted 1969.

The Osborne Collection of Early Children's Books 1566-1910. A catalogue. Toronto Public Library, 1958; new edition in three volumes, 1975-9.

Two useful general books, two excellent illustrated books by a noted collector and two interesting monographs:

Hobbs, A. S., and Whalley, J. I. *Beatrix Potter.* Victoria and Albert Museum, 1985.

Quayle, E. *The Collector's Book of Children's Books.* Studio Vista, [1971].

Quayle, E. *The Collector's Book of Boy's Stories.* Studio Vista, 1973.

Schuster, T., and Engen, R. *Printed Kate Greenaway.* A catalogue raisonné. Schuster Gallery, 1986.

Whalley, J. I., and Chester, T. R. *The Oxford Companion to Children's Literature.* Oxford University Press, 1984.

Whalley, J. I., and Chester, T. R. *A History of Children's Book Illustration.* Victoria and Albert Museum, 1988.

There are also bibliographies of Lear and Carroll. Information on children's illustrators may be found in Bland and Houfe (see under chapter 9).

Chapter 7: Bindings

Craft bookbindings:

Middleton, B. *A History of English Craft Bookbinding Technique.* British Library, new edition 1996.

Nixon, H. *Five Centuries of English Bookbindings.* Scolar Press, revised edition 1979.

Publisher's bindings:

Carter, J. *Publisher's Cloth, 1820-1900.* Constable, 1938.

McLean, R. *Victorian Publisher's Book-Bindings in Cloth and Leather.* Gordon Fraser, 1974.

McLean, R. *Victorian Publisher's Book-Bindings in Paper.* Gordon Fraser, 1983.

Lists of binders with their dates:

Howe, E. *A List of London Bookbinders, 1648-1815.* Batsford, reprinted 1988.

Ramsden, C. *London Book Binders, 1780-1840.* Batsford, reprinted 1987.

Ramsden, C. *Bookbinders of the UK (outside London) 1780-1840.* Batsford, reprinted 1989.

Also:

Baker, J. *Mauchline Ware.* Shire, Princes Risborough, 1985.

Foot, M. *Pictorial Bookbindings.* British Library, 1986.

Chapter 8: Press books

Chambers, D. *18th and 19th Century Private Presses*. Private Libraries Association, 1997.

Dreyfus, J. *A History of the Nonesuch Press*. Nonesuch Press, 1981.

Franklin, C. *The Private Presses*. 1969; new edition, Studio Vista, 1990.

Peterson, W. S. *The Kelmscott Press*. Oxford University Press, 1991.

The Golden Cockerel Press has issued bibliographies of its books: *Chanticleer, Pertelote, Cockalorum and Cock-a-hoop.*

Chapter 9: Illustrated books

Balston, T. *English Wood-Engraving, 1900-1950*. Art & Technics, 1951.

Bland, D. *A History of Book Illustration*. Faber, second edition 1969.

Harthan, J. *The History of the Illustrated Book*. Thames & Hudson, 1981.

Horne, A. *Dictionary of 20th Century British Book Illustrators*. Antique Collector's Club, reprinted 1995.

Houfe, S. *Dictionary of 19th Century British Book Illustrators, 1800-1914*. Antique Collector's Club, new edition 1996.

Hunnisett, B. *An Illustrated Dictionary of British Steel Engravers*. Scolar Press, revised edition 1989.

Muir, P. *Victorian Illustrated Books*. Batsford, reprinted 1985.

See also Abbey and Tooley (chapter 5). A bibliography of the A. & C. Black books by C. Inman has been published by Werner Shaw, 1990.

Chapter 10: Popular editions and series

For 'Yellowbacks' see an important contribution in Sadleir (chapter 4).

Carney, M. *Britain in Pictures, a History and Bibliography*. Werner Shaw, 1996.

Holme, C. (editor). *The Studio. A Bibliography of the First Fifty Years, 1893-1943*. The Studio, 1978.

Rotheroe, J. (editor). *30 Years of Shire Publications*. Shire, 1992.

Todd, W. B., and Bowden, A. *Tauchnitz International Editions in English, 1841-1955*. New York, 1988.

Williams, W. E. *The Penguin Story*. Allen Lane, 1956.

Chapter 11: Modern first editions

Connolly, J. *Modern First Editions. Their Value to Collectors*. Little, Brown, New York, 1996.

The Soho (now Oxford University Press) and St Paul's (now Oak Knoll Press) bibliographies have between them published monographic bibliographies of Churchill, Shaw, Woolf, the Sitwells, Pound, Forster, Greene, Conan Doyle *et al.*, and practically all well-known twentieth-century authors have their own bibiliography. If your local library cannot help in tracing it, the excellent staff at the Book Trust (telephone: 0181-874 8526) almost certainly will.

Baker, J. *The Low Cost of Bookloving*. Reader's Union, 1958. About the Readers' Union book club.

Chapter 12: Ideas.

Arber, A. *Herbals, Their Origin and Evolution.* Cambridge University Press, revised edition 1986.

Bondy, L. *Miniature Books.* Richard Joseph, reprint 1994.

Desmond, R. *Bibliography of British Gardens.* St Paul's Bibliographies, Winchester, 1988.

Donovan, R. E., and Murdoch, J. *The Game of Golf and the Printed Word 1566-1985.* Castalio Press, New York, 1987.

Driver, E. *Bibliography of Cookery Books Published in Britain, 1875-1914.* Prospect Books, reprint 1996.

Enser, A. G. S. *Filmed Books and Plays, 1926-89.* Gower, Aldershot, revised edition 1989.

Freeman, R. B. *British Natural History Books, 1496-1900, a Handlist.* Dawson, 1980.

Gernsheim, H. *Incunabula of British Photography, a Bibiliography 1839-75.* 1984.

Henrey, B. *British Botanical and Horticultural Literature before 1800.* Oxford University Press, three volumes, 1975.

Hopkinson, C. *Collecting Golf Books, 1743-1938.* Constable, 1938.

Knight, D. *Natural Science Books in English.* Batsford, 1972.

Mullens, W. H., and Swann, K. *Bibliography of British Ornithology. Earliest Times to 1912.* 1917; Wheldon & Wesley, reprint 1986.

Chapter 13: Glossary of terms

Carter, J. *ABC for Book Collectors.* 1952; new edition, revised and enlarged, Werner Shaw, 1996. The classic work.

Glaister, G. *Encyclopedia of the Book.* The British Library, 1996.

General books on the history of books and book collecting

Carter, J. *Taste and Technique in Book Collecting.* Private Libraries Association, revised edition 1997.

Carter, J., and Muir, P., *et al.* (editors). *Printing and the Mind of Man.* 1965; new edition enlarged, Karl Pressler, München, 1983. A much respected, and quoted, catalogue of pioneering works in all fields of human endeavour.

Clair, C. *A Chronology of Printing.* Cassell, 1969.

Laverie, N. *The Art and History of Books.* British Library, 1995.

Reynolds Stone's wood engraving for a famous reference book, 1965.

Millar, S. *Book Collecting*. Provincial Booksellers Fairs Association, 1994.
Thomas, A. *Great Books and Book Collectors*. Weidenfeld & Nicolson, 1975.
Uden, G. *Understanding Book Collecting*. Antique Collector's Club, 1996.

An important reference catalogue of the holdings of the British Library (then part of the British Museum):

British Museum General Catalogue of Printed Books to 1955 (with supplements). Readex Microprint Corp, New York, compact edition 1967.

Periodicals

Two scholarly quarterlies:
> *The Book Collector*
> *The Library*

and three livelier monthlies:
> *Antiquarian Book Monthly*
> *Book Collector*
> *Biblio* (American, but available in the UK).

Names and addresses of booksellers in your area (with their specialities, if any) and information on book fairs may be obtained from the Antiquarian Booksellers Association, Sackville House, 40 Piccadilly, London W1V 9PA (telephone: 0171-439 3118), the Provincial Booksellers Fairs Association, The Old Coach House, 16 Melbourne Street, Royston, Hertfordshire SG8 7BZ (telephone: 01763 248400) or from *Sheppard's Directory of Secondhand Book Dealers in the British Isles* (revised yearly), Richard Joseph Publishers Ltd.

Index